COLLECTED PLAYS FOR CHILDREN

also by Ted Hughes

poetry
THE HAWK IN THE RAIN
LUPERCAL
WODWO
CROW
GAUDETE
FLOWERS AND INSECTS
MOORTOWN
MOORTOWN DIARY
WOLFWATCHING
RAIN-CHARM FOR THE DUCHY
THREE BOOKS: Remains of Elmet, Cave Birds, River
ELMET (with photographs by Fay Godwin)
NEW SELECTED POEMS 1957–1994
TALES FROM OVID
BIRTHDAY LETTERS
COLLECTED POEMS

SENECA'S OEDIPUS
WEDEKIND'S SPRING AWAKENING
LORCA'S BLOOD WEDDING
RACINE'S PHÈDRE
THE ORESTEIA OF AESCHYLUS
EURIPIDES' ALCESTIS
SELECTED POEMS OF EMILY DICKINSON
SELECTED VERSE OF SHAKESPEARE
A CHOICE OF COLERIDGE'S VERSE
THE RATTLE BAG (edited with Seamus Heaney)
THE SCHOOL BAG (edited with Seamus Heaney)
BY HEART: 101 Poems to Remember

prose
POETRY IN THE MAKING
A DANCER TO GOD
SHAKESPEARE AND THE GODDESS OF COMPLETE BEING
WINTER POLLEN: Occasional Prose
DIFFICULTIES OF A BRIDEGROOM

for children
HOW THE WHALE BECAME
MEET MY FOLKS!
THE EARTH-OWL AND OTHER MOON PEOPLE
NESSIE, THE MANNERLESS MONSTER
THE IRON MAN
MOON-WHALES
SEASON SONGS
UNDER THE NORTH STAR
FFANGS THE VAMPIRE BAT AND THE KISS OF TRUTH
TALES OF THE EARLY WORLD
THE IRON WOMAN
THE DREAMFIGHTER AND OTHER CREATION TALES
COLLECTED ANIMAL POEMS Vols. 1–4
SHAGGY AND SPOTTY
THE MERMAID'S PURSE
THE CAT AND THE CUCKOO

Collected Plays for Children

TED HUGHES

faber and faber

First published in 2001
by Faber and Faber Limited
3 Queen Square London WC1N 3AU

Typeset by RefineCatch Limited, Bungay, Suffolk
Printed in England by Mackays of Chatham plc, Chatham, Kent

A CIP record for this book
is available from the British Library

ISBN 0-571-20957-2

2 4 6 8 10 9 7 5 3

THE COMING OF THE KINGS

CHARACTERS

THE FORTUNE-TELLER
THE INNKEEPER
HIS WIFE
THE PRIEST
THE BUSINESSMAN
THE POLICE INSPECTOR
THE MINSTREL
JOSEPH
MARY
THE THREE KINGS

THE COMING OF THE KINGS

*The road leads in from the right-back, towards the
audience, dividing the inn, on the left, from the
tumbledown animal shed on the right. The inn is red,
with white door and window frames. Out over the door
hangs a large sign:* THE EMPEROR'S HEAD, *from which
dangles a giant reproduction of a Roman coin, with a
head crudely painted on it. The cottage is black, with
loose sacking over the windows and the door which,
lifted aside, would reveal most of the interior.*

A cock crows.
The FORTUNE-TELLER *appears, trudging down the
road towards the audience. He stops, yawns, shifts his
pack. At that moment, a deafening commotion from the
shed on the right: kicking sounds, violent bangs, and the
prolonged lusty braying of a donkey.* FORTUNE-
TELLER *drops his pack in surprise, stares at the shed in
amazement. Bedroom window of the inn slams open,
innkeeper's* WIFE's *head appears: she yells at the top of
her voice.*

WIFE: All night long you've been at it!
When will you shut up your racket!
Shut up, you ugly brute, you!
Or I'll get my husband to shoot you.
*The donkey is silenced. Her head disappears and the
window whams shut. The* FORTUNE-TELLER *looks to
and fro between the shed and the inn.*
He tiptoes towards the shed, listens.
An ox lows.
The FORTUNE-TELLER *starts, listens again.*
FORTUNE-TELLER: What's that? What did you say?

[3]

(*Ox lows.*)
What? Here? Today?
(*Ox lows.*)
That's what I thought you said.
(*Ox lows.*)
Oh, my poor head!
But that's incredible!
(*Cock crows.*)
What's that? You say it's true?
(*Dog barks.*)
You too? You too?
Oh, now what shall I do!
Donkey begins to bray and kick up a tremendous din.
Inn door opens, and out comes the INNKEEPER *in his*
nightcap and nightshirt, waving a thick stick. Bedroom
window opens and his WIFE's *head sticks out.*

WIFE: Batter the brute with your stick
    Till where he's thin he goes thick
    And where he's thick he goes thin.
    Silence the monster's din.
    I haven't had a wink all night . . .
    No wonder I look such a sight.

FORTUNE-TELLER: Stop! What will you do?

INNKEEPER: I'll hammer the donkey black and blue
    And the ox I'll hammer pink.
    All night we've not had a wink
    For their mooing and creaking and braying . . .

FORTUNE-TELLER: But don't you hear what they're saying?

INNKEEPER: Saying? Are you right in the head?

FORTUNE-TELLER: Didn't you hear what the donkey said?

INNKEEPER: Now you're a peculiar feller!

WIFE: Is that that fortune-teller?

FORTUNE-TELLER: Madame, at your service. If you've a

[4]

wrinkle in your palm, I'll read it: there's health, wealth
and beauty in wrinkles, if you get the right man to read
them. The more wrinkles you have, the more there is to
read for your fortune, so the more fortune for you. That's
a lucky face, lady.

WIFE: I've heard of you. Wait. I'll be down.

Her head disappears.

INNKEEPER: Have you just arrived in town?

FORTUNE-TELLER: I know where the money lies.

INNKEEPER: Well, this town has plenty of flies.

But money? Think again.

I have to scrape like a hen.

I've had to sell my brother for a slave.

It's so difficult here to save.

Enter WIFE *from inn.*

WIFE: Fortune-teller!

FORTUNE-TELLER: Madame!

WIFE: Oh, please read my palm.

What does it say, quick? Oh, I feel funny.

FORTUNE-TELLER: First, you cross my palm with money.

WIFE: How much?

FORTUNE-TELLER: Let it be silver.

INNKEEPER: *Stop!*

WIFE *turns on her husband furiously, while*
FORTUNE-TELLER *holds and inspects her palm.*

WIFE: Have you mended my wobbly mop?

Have you nailed the carpet down?

Or flattened the nail that catches in my gown?

Or oiled the door and the kitchen pump?

What are you standing there for, you lump?

INNKEEPER: Week in week out, and never a guest,

And you give silver to this pest?

WIFE: Then why did you want to keep an inn?

Think of the lady I might have been
If you'd had guts enough to launch
That pudding barrel elephant paunch
Into some trade with better . . .

FORTUNE-TELLER: Money!

WIFE: What?

INNKEEPER: What's that?

FORTUNE-TELLER: I read here
That the greatest good luck in a million year
Is coming your way.

INNKEEPER: What? Where? *When*?

FORTUNE-TELLER (*still studying the* WIFE's *palm*): Today.

WIFE: Today?

FORTUNE-TELLER: The King Of Men
Is going to visit your inn – today.

INNKEEPER: What? What's that? What do you say?

FORTUNE-TELLER: Be prepared.

INNKEEPER: A king?

FORTUNE-TELLER: *Three* kings.

INNKEEPER: Beyond my wildest imaginings!
To stay with us here?

FORTUNE-TELLER: To visit this inn.
A new age is going to begin
From what occurs at this inn today.
And you will be famous for ever.

WIFE: For ever!

INNKEEPER: Now who's stupid? Now who's clever?
I bought this inn ten years ago
For this moment. What else do you know?

FORTUNE-TELLER: Prepare.

WIFE: Three kings!

INNKEEPER: When we've had them,
Every night after, we'll be crammed full.

We'll be on the map, the fashionable
Most famous inn in Bethlehem.
We'll make a fortune!

WIFE (*in great excitement*): Get the place clean.
Some of those rooms aren't fit to be seen.
Scrub them, sweep them, quick, quick, quick, and
Get the flea-powder.

INNKEEPER: Get the chickens
Out of the bath.

WIFE: Get all the dogs
And their pups out of the beds and the hogs
And the hoglets out of the cupboards and scatter
Disinfectant. What's the matter?

INNKEEPER (*he is standing almost in a trance*): This is the
greatest day of my life!

WIFE: And as usual you've to thank your wife.
Get a move on.

They dash into the inn. Through what follows the WIFE
*is throwing bundles of rags, broken chairs, picture
frames, etc. out of the windows. Soon the* INNKEEPER
*re-emerges dressed and begins to carry the junk into the
shed. But first:*

FORTUNE-TELLER: I told them no more than the true.
But I have not told it all.
A cloud wrote on the blue
That a world is about to fall
Out of mind and care;
Along with the rest, these two:
This penny-shoveller,
His ghost shall be trapped in the bell
Of a grocer's till, and shall cry
Every sale with a yell
Of envious agony:

[7]

Throughout eternity
That shall be his Hell.
And his grasping wife
Who would have beaten the ass,
She shall stare eternity out
Trapped in a looking-glass.
Exit the FORTUNE-TELLER.
Enter the INNKEEPER, *loads himself with flotsam.*

INNKEEPER: The lazy dog will miss his chance,
But the ambitious dog will dance
And so will I. When luck arrives
It's the ready man who thrives.
Others awake when it's flown past . . .
But I'm the ready man at last.
I shall not miss it, I shall not miss it!
I'll catch it by the wings and kiss it.
WIFE *throws down a basketwork cradle from the bedroom, it hits him.*

WIFE: Dump this old cradle into the shed.
Have you fixed the attic bed?
(*She continues until he has flung all the rubbish into the shed and scurried back into the inn.*)
Have you polished the brass door-knobs?
There are about a thousand jobs.
Have you scrubbed the table-top?
A new hinge on the cellar-drop?
Have you brought the barrels up?
Hurry up! Hurry up! Hurry up! Hurry up!

INNKEEPER: Yes, yes, yes . . .
(*He is about to re-enter the inn when he stops, stares. A priest in sumptuous robes enters.*)
Er – Your Majes – er, Your Lordship – er, Your
Honour . . .

[8]

PRIEST: Your Grace.

INNKEEPER: Your Grace?

PRIEST: As you see, I'm a high priest of the temple.

My means and my spirituality are equally ample.

That is to say . . . I'm a power on earth, and in heaven.

That is to say . . . do you follow me? Yes?

INNKEEPER: Your Grace.

He bows, he kneels, he bumps his forehead on the ground.

PRIEST (*pompous*): No need to bang your head so hard on the street.

It's quite enough if you kneel. Both knees. I repeat:

When you look at me, do you feel yourself quake?

That's the devil in you. I'm more than he can take.

You know the most evil things in this world, what they are?

They are troublesome new religious ideas. Heavens! I could swear,

I could curse the ears off an elephant,

When I think of the wickedness of people!

(*He grows enraged.*)

I will not permit them to think whatever they want,

I want their souls, I tell you, tethered to my steeple.

I want them in my fold. In my power.

I will not let them out of my grasp. I want to see them cower

Under the purity of my glare

When I see them sitting so wicked there!

Oh!

INNKEEPER: Yes, Your Grace.

PRIEST: And now do you know what's come to my ear?

An illegal religious festival is going to be held. Here.

Well?

[9]

INNKEEPER: Your Grace, I –

PRIEST: The wickedness! The wickedness!
　　People think they can have heavenly happiness
　　Without my permission. They want to be able to pray
　　Without paying me money! Though my money's all
　　　　taken away
　　By Great Herod to pay for his army.

INNKEEPER: Your Grace –

PRIEST: Where are the vandals? Don't deny it to my face.

INNKEEPER: Your Grace – I don't know what you're talking
　　about.

PRIEST: You say so. Very well. I shall stay. I shall sit them out.
　　I'll stay here in your inn till I hear their revels,
　　Then I'll descend in the Hand of God and cast out their
　　　　devils
　　And deliver them over to Herod who knows full well
　　That these new religions come from Hell.
　　Lead me to a room.

INNKEEPER (*scrambling up*): Your Grace.

PRIEST: And bring me wine.
　　And bring me roasted quails. I might as well dine.
　　PRIEST *follows the* INNKEEPER *into the inn.*
　　Enter, in a bowler, and humming 'Three Blind Mice', a
　　BUSINESSMAN. *He studies the inn.*
　　Re-enter INNKEEPER *and* WIFE, *in great excitement.*

WIFE: What's he talking about?

INNKEEPER: I don't *know.*

WIFE: Illegal religious festival?

INNKEEPER: He says *so.*

WIFE: But whatever can he mean?

INNKEEPER: That's it. What can he mean?

WIFE: And is he paying for the wine?

INNKEEPER: We'll send him the bill.

WIFE: But he's a great man. He'll advertise us, he will.
    I mean, just by being here. Get him his quails.
INNKEEPER: I've sent. We must put on a great banquet, for if
    today's fails –
WIFE: Don't you see? It's beginning. Our luck's begun.
INNKEEPER: O let me be wealthy for ever before today's
    done.
WIFE: Get about it, you idiot.
    She goes, he stands, calculating on his fingers the items he
    needs to remember, flustered and pressed.
BUSINESSMAN: So this is 'The Emperor's Head'. Then this is
    the one.
INNKEEPER (*startled*):Your Grace?
BUSINESSMAN: What?
INNKEEPER: I mean, sir, is there –
BUSINESSMAN: Tell me, my good man,
    I've heard there's going to be a world-famous magician
    Performing an earth-shaking exhibition
    Of miracles here today. Have you heard?
INNKEEPER: Magician? Here? Today? Not a word.
BUSINESSMAN: One of those Holy Men who walk on fire,
    Tie venomous snakes in knots without any fear,
    Turn a sardine into a cartload of cod,
    Bring the rain down like Almighty God,
    Convert a crust of bread into a whole field of barley –
    One of those holy wonders. Maybe I'm a bit early –
INNKEEPER: I've heard nothing about it, sir.
BUSINESSMAN: Come, come,
    Some rival interest's paid you to keep mum.
    Eh?
INNKEEPER: Rival interest?
BUSINESSMAN: Well, well, well.
    Don't think I'm going to be fooled. It's valuable –

A show like this. I sign him on, see?
Wait a minute, maybe you don't know me.

INNKEEPER: I'm afraid, sir, er, I . . .

BUSINESSMAN: Socrates D. Conkhorse.
I'll sell anything – reasonable of course.
I don't try to sell the moon, though some would buy.
You must understand, I'm a plain honest guy.
I sell untried gladiators by tens,
Rope sandals by millions, dwarfs with wens
By the brace. Would you like a crocodile?
Or a beautiful slave-girl plus the coconut isle?
Cash down and it's yours.

INNKEEPER: As a matter of fact, my sandals are a bit
frayed –

BUSINESSMAN: And with this miracle-worker, I'm made!
A man who can raise the dead! That's really new!
I sign him on at forty per cent and – phew!
It makes me sweat to think of the fortune going.
Look, five per cent for you, just for showing
Where he's lodging.

INNKEEPER: But I don't quite see –

BUSINESSMAN: Look: ten pounds, and he'll raise your aunt
or your uncle. Agree?
A hundred pounds to raise a grandad. Three
Thousand to raise a father. There's no limit!
Don't you want to make a fortune, dammit?
Where is he? O.K. You're going to play dumb?
Well, I'll stay here in this hotel till he's come.
I'll hear him by his crowd.

INNKEEPER: You can stay gladly.

BUSINESSMAN: But understand, I think you've served me
badly.
Bring me some beer in, and I'd like some beef.

INNKEEPER: Straight ahead, sir.

As the INNKEEPER *and the* BUSINESSMAN *enter the inn
a* POLICE INSPECTOR *saunters in, stops, surveys the
shed and the inn, consulting his notebook. Re-enter the*
INNKEEPER *and his* WIFE *talking together excitedly.*

WIFE: It's beyond belief.

INNKEEPER: We've never had such guests in our lives.

WIFE: Fortune comes to the one who believes

All that the Fortune-teller says.

INNKEEPER: I'll have to run down into the town.

We need more food. Oh, day of days!

WIFE: Hurry up and get it, you clown!

WIFE re-enters the inn, the INNKEEPER *is about to dash
off when he sees the* POLICE INSPECTOR.

POLICE INSPECTOR: The Emperor's Head. Hm!

(*Consulting his book.*)

Opposite, a shed

Of god-forsaken ruinous aspect. The shed!

This must be the place. Hm!

(*Shuts his book.*)

And you're the proprietor?

INNKEEPER: That's right, Inspector. Anything wrong?

POLICE INSPECTOR: We haven't met before?

INNKEEPER: No.

POLICE INSPECTOR: Sure?

INNKEEPER: Yes.

POLICE INSPECTOR: What are your politics?

INNKEEPER: I haven't any.

POLICE INSPECTOR: Be careful.

INNKEEPER: I agree with all tax.

POLICE INSPECTOR: Good for you. Well, well, and who'd
have thought!

INNKEEPER: What's wrong, Inspector?

POLICE INSPECTOR: Who's staying with you? Straight out,
    Don't stop to invent a lie.
INNKEEPER: Guests?
POLICE INSPECTOR: Who?
INNKEEPER: A high priest of the Temple. And a businessman.
    Just two.
POLICE INSPECTOR: And what do you know about this
    demonstration?
    Don't put on that dumbfounded, ox-like expression.
    It's been brought to our notice that today
    A Political Agitator is going to say his say
    Here at 'The Emperor's Head', and threaten our state
    With red-hot ideas, turbulence of passion
    To shake our law and order out of fashion,
    Make people discontented with their noses,
    And shoot at policemen, and trample the palace roses
    With peering in at the windows carrying knives.
    Herod's court are in terror of their lives.
    What have you to say?
INNKEEPER: Me? I'm just an innkeeper.
POLICE INSPECTOR: Politically, you're a dangerous sleeper.
    It's men like you who let the matches catch,
    Who let the fireflies of rebellion hatch.
INNKEEPER: I don't know what you're talking about.
POLICE INSPECTOR: Well then,
    Where is the crowd assembled to hear this man?
INNKEEPER: Which man?
POLICE INSPECTOR: This revolutionary with his message for
    the people which
    Is going to shake Herod and cause a hitch
    In the smooth running of great Caesar's lands?
    I've got to catch him. Stop wringing your hands.
INNKEEPER: I just don't know what all this is about.

[14]

POLICE INSPECTOR: Haven't you seen some bearded
  ferocious figure
  With a dagger like a bread-knife only bigger,
  Whispering to a dozen like himself?
  He wants to topple Herod off the shelf.
  I can't decide whether you're innocent
  Or only bluffing.

INNKEEPER: Please, Inspector, don't.
  I don't know what's come over me today.
  I hardly understand what people say.

POLICE INSPECTOR: All right then. I'll stay here, in your
  pleasant inn.
  And when this fellow's followers begin
  To gather to hear him speak – I shall be peeping.
  Today, the State's safety is in my keeping.
  Show me a room.

INNKEEPER: Certainly, Inspector.

POLICE INSPECTOR: If this man's the disease, then I'm the
  doctor.
  Bring me a barrel of wine and a boar's head.
  I'll fix a hundred of them when I've fed.
  Exit the INNKEEPER *with the* POLICE INSPECTOR.
  Enter the wandering MINSTREL, *in beggarly raiment.*
  He stands looking at the shed. He lifts the sacking
  and peers in.
  Re-enter INNKEEPER *and his* WIFE, *excited as before.*

INNKEEPER: It's beyond me.

WIFE: Three of them!

INNKEEPER: The Great of Jerusalem!

WIFE: But *three.*

INNKEEPER: Yes, and the greatest!

WIFE: *Three.*

INNKEEPER: This Inspector, the latest,

He fairly made me sweat!
Now they're downing all they can get.
The High Priest's drunk a crate.
He's joined with the businessman.
But what do they all mean?
What are they waiting for?
One man, or three, or more?
An illegal religious meeting?
A fire-walking, fire-eating
Magician, or a revolt?
I'm sure it's not my fault.

WIFE: I've got it!

INNKEEPER: What?

WIFE: Three!

INNKEEPER: What do you mean? I don't see.

WIFE: The three kings are these three.
The Fortune-teller told
There would be Three, and – behold.

INNKEEPER: These three are kings?

WIFE: Aren't they?

INNKEEPER: Disguised, do you mean to say?

WIFE (*dancing*): Kings! Kings!
What wonderful creatures are kings!

INNKEEPER (*still incredulous*): And we've got a houseful?

WIFE: Isn't it blissful?

INNKEEPER (*suddenly going wild*): We shall make a fortune!
We're made!
They'll say: 'That's where *They* stayed.'

BOTH: Kings! Kings! O wonderful things . . .

*They dance around together, but break apart seeing
the* MINSTREL.

INNKEEPER: Who's that? What's he doing peering into my
old stable?

[16]

The MINSTREL *comes forward, as if not seeing the two.*

MINSTREL: The hills were against me.

    The sharp, peevish edges of the road-stones were against me,

    And the thorns were against me,

    But I made my way.

    The dogs were with me, one brought me a ham-bone.

    The birds were with me and showed me fresh eggs,

    And the stream, the stream

    Came out of its way to clear itself at my feet.

    By these signs a traveller knows

    The moving spirits are friendly.

    And here is the place: The Emperor's Head.

    The Emperor's head that spoke to me in a dream –

INNKEEPER: Hey, you, rags, what do you want?

MINSTREL: Food and a bed.

    I have come a long way with a fever in my head.

INNKEEPER: Do you know where you are?

MINSTREL: I am under the sun, the god-given day-star.

INNKEEPER: Don't you know where you're standing?

MINSTREL: On an earth of the Creator's making and lending.

INNKEEPER: Do you know who you're speaking to?

WIFE: Yes, just whose pig-keeper are you?

    Your toes are insulting the sky.

    The birds have slept in your hair.

    Your trousers are ready to die,

    Your coat's only just there.

    You're like a rat's nest walking.

    Are you begging or hawking?

MINSTREL: Any bed and a slice of bread

    To keep the soul in my body, lady.

TED HUGHES

WIFE: Away with you, you rubbish heap.
  This is an inn where Great Kings sleep.
  He's one of those disreputable minstrels.
  Upper window opens, PRIEST'*s head appears.*
PRIEST: More wine up here! Service! Do you hear?
  BUSINESSMAN'*s head appears.*
BUSINESSMAN: Get more beef up and more beer.
WIFE: Coming, sir.
  She runs into the inn.
INNKEEPER: Well, you heard that.
  Now what are you staring at?
MINSTREL: Look at that star.
INNKEEPER: It's only a star.
MINSTREL: But it's shining by day.
  Upper window opens again and the WIFE'*s angry head
  sticks out.*
WIFE: There you still are!
  Hurry up, man. More food and more drink.
  Don't stand gaping like the kitchen sink.
  The head vanishes and the window bangs.
INNKEEPER: You'd better be off. And I'd better hurry.
  As you see, we're full up. I'm sorry.
  INNKEEPER *runs off.* MINSTREL *stands as he was.*
MINSTREL: What a King of Men is Greedy!
  Penny calls to penny, stronger than a man.
  Floors call to carpets, stronger than a man.
  Tables call to linen, stronger than a man.
  Walls call to paintings, stronger than a man.
  For a man's mind is money's slave.

  The poor torn coat calls to the silk lining,
  The old split bowl to figured silver,
  The dirty dry glass to the vineyards

The rough bread calls to the sturgeon –
And a man goes running their errands
For a man's mind is money's slave.

Bow down, bow down and worship
The big belly of the cash-bank
That has swallowed so many slaves.
May you all go to the heaven
Of a crumbling junk-heap.
(*During this the stage has darkened: he turns to the
shed.*)
Now night falls on the mountain valleys and in the
   gardens.
Now the cold comes down
Murdering the small birds in their feathers as they
   sleep.
The fish in ponds lose consciousness with the cold.
I'll creep in here and the breath of an ox and a donkey
Will do me for blankets. These are hard times
For those who cannot persuade themselves to rob.
He goes into the shed.
*The three guests are singing 'Three Blind Mice' as a
round-song.*
JOSEPH *and* MARY *come up the road and stop in front of
the inn.*

JOSEPH: We have come a long way. We can't go farther
   tonight, in the cold. The snow is beginning to prickle
   our faces. If this inn's full up, the Lord knows what we
   shall do. I'll knock.

   JOSEPH *knocks. The* INNKEEPER *comes scampering
   up, returning from his errand of ordering more food.
   He doesn't notice that* JOSEPH *has knocked.*

INNKEEPER: Brrr! What a night! Hello – is your wife ill?

She looks as if she might need a doctor. You ought
to look after her, old man.
(*He speaks to audience.*)
These people who wander about the roads are terrible.
They treat each other like rats and mice: no feelings at
all. Brr!
He goes in, shuts the door.

JOSEPH: I'll try again.
(*He knocks.* WIFE *looks out.*)
We need a room. And my wife here needs a bed.

WIFE: Sorry, full up.
She bangs the door to.

JOSEPH: Now what shall we do?
Door opens, the INNKEEPER *comes out.*

INNKEEPER: I'm terribly sorry. I think I ought to explain.
You see that sign: it says 'The Emperor's Head'.
That is to say, it's a hostel for Emperors – Kings.
Kings as Kings, or incognito Kings.
Those three fine voices come from the throats of
    Kings
Who may well be pretending not to be Kings.
And I'm reserving three rooms for three Kings
Who whether they come disguised or else as Kings
Will still demand I treat them all as Kings.
And can a man of my sort deny Kings?
Kings made me, and Kings keep me. I am the King's.
You understand? You can sleep in that shed.
You do understand that I can't do differently?
He runs back into the hotel.

JOSEPH: We're out of luck. Go in.
*They go into the shed. 'Three Blind Mice' rises and falls
away.*
'We Three Kings' heard faintly in the distance.

'Three Blind Mice' rises again, falls away behind what
follows.
Enter INNKEEPER *and his* WIFE *arguing.*

INNKEEPER: But if these are Kings we could be renting
The three empty rooms. Two here were wanting
A room just now. And they'd have paid.

WIFE: And if they're not Kings, but just what they said?
Then the three Kings will be coming tonight.
The Fortune-teller's proving right
In everything else, so why not in this?
We can't afford to miss what we'd miss.
Those three rooms must be kept for the Kings
Who will be coming if these are not Kings.
I'm freezing. Anyway you're wrong. These *are* the Kings.

INNKEEPER: They don't behave much like Kings.

WIFE: Do you mean because they're blotto?
'The customer's always right' is my motto.
Bring up more wine, in case more Kings come.
You are so unbelievably dumb.

She goes in, INNKEEPER *runs in after.*

INNKEEPER: I'm only afraid I'm losing money!

'We Three Kings' is now quite loud.

MINSTREL *comes staggering out of the shed, shaking his*
head, rousing himself. He stands, collecting his wits.
Something amazing has happened to him.

MINSTREL: I've just had an astounding dream as I lay in the
straw.
I dreamed a star fell on to the straw beside me
And lay blazing. Then when I looked up
I saw a bull come flying through a sky of fire
And on its shoulders a huge silver woman
Holding the moon. And afterwards there came
A donkey flying through that same burning heaven

[21]

And on its shoulders a colossal man
Holding the sun. Suddenly I awoke
And saw a bull and a donkey kneeling in the straw,
And the great moving shadows of a man and a woman –
I say they were a man and a woman but
I dare not say what I think they were. I did not dare to
    look.
I ran out here into the freezing world
Because I dared not look. Inside that shed.
As he turns to look at the shed, he sees something down
the road where before he had seen the star by day. The
INNKEEPER *comes out of the inn, pausing in the open*
doorway.

INNKEEPER: What do you say?
WIFE: I said get more logs.
INNKEEPER: I heard. I have only a man's legs.
    I don't have a stag's or a running dog's.
    (*Now to the* MINSTREL.)
    What's the matter with you?
    You look so white you look blue.
    What are you staring at?
MINSTREL: Look.
    INNKEEPER *follows the direction of* MINSTREL'S
    finger, stares, then drops the log basket he is carrying
    and bolts into the inn.
INNKEEPER: Wife! Wife! Quick! Look at this!
MINSTREL: A star is coming this way along the road.
    If I were not standing upright, this would be a dream.
    A star the shape of a sword of fire, point-downward,
    Is floating along the road. And now it rises.
    It is shaking fire on to the roofs and the gardens.
    (*Star appears, suspended, rising slowly from behind till it*
    comes to rest directly over the animal shed.)

And now it rises above the animal shed
Where I slept till the dream woke me. And now
The star is standing over the animal shed.
During this speech, as the star rose to its position, a light
kindled within the shed, and now light is beaming from
every crevice.
'We Three Kings' *at full volume, so much as may not*
drown the speech.
Re-enter, from the inn, INNKEEPER *and* WIFE. *He points*
not at the star but down the road up which it has come.

INNKEEPER: Look, if those are not three Kings, I'm a turnip.

WIFE: Oh, bless that Fortune-teller. It's the Kings.

Enter, majestically, fully arrayed, the three KINGS.
INNKEEPER *and his* WIFE *fall on their knees.*

INNKEEPER: This way, Your Majesties.

Everything's prepared for your ease.

A banquet to tickle your eyes.

WIFE: We're roasting a dozen sucking pigs.

INNKEEPER: We're basting them with brandied figs.

WIFE: We've hired a little orchestra

To help you down the vintage-jar.

INNKEEPER: Our motto is 'Guests, stuff your gullets

Till your buttons fly like bullets' –

Er – Your Majesties – this – this

This is the inn. Your Majesties!

That's only a horrible old place where I keep my donkey
and my old bull and my rubbish – Your Majesties!

The three KINGS *ignore the inn and the* INNKEEPER,
their attention is on the stable.

FIRST KING: We have followed the star over mountains

Where the stones cried and the thorns were broken.

We have followed the star over deserts

Where the rocks split at the touch of the night cold,

We have followed the beckoning of that star
Till it stands where it stands. We have arrived.
SECOND KING: He will be born to the coughing of animals
Among the broken, rejected objects
In the corner that costs not a penny
In the darkness of the mouse and the spider.
The THIRD KING *has lifted aside the sacking front of*
the shed.
THIRD KING: He is here. The King of the Three Worlds
Has been born and is here.
The three KINGS *enter the shed, leaving the sacking*
wide, the light blazing out from the interior.
Snow has started to fall and is now coming down in
thick windless flakes.
'Once in Royal David's City' begins softly, taking over
from 'We Three Kings' which faded as they spoke.
INNKEEPER *and his* WIFE *are still kneeling.*
INNKEEPER: What? What are they saying? Where are they
going? Who's been born? What's happening?
Why are the Three Great Kings going into my old stable?
Why is that star standing over the roof of my old stable?
Who has lit that great light inside my old stable?
What is happening? Why doesn't somebody tell me?
What's going on in my old stable?
'Once in Royal David's City' now loud. MINSTREL
stands in stage-centre, under the thickly falling snow.
MINSTREL: Listen. The snow is falling.
Snow is falling on all the roads.
Falling on to the hills, on to the eyelashes of sheep.
Falling into the chimneys and on to the doorsteps,
Into the frozen well, into the dark forest.
Slowly the heavens are falling.
Every snowflake is an angel.

The angels are settling on the world.
The world will be white with angels.
The world will be deep in angels.
'Once in Royal David's City' now very loud. The
MINSTREL *stands in the large falling flakes. The*
INNKEEPER *and his* WIFE, *as they were, bewildered and*
overawed, kneel in the snow. The manger scene is
silhouetted in the great golden light beaming from the
stable under the large bright star.

THE TIGER'S BONES

CHARACTERS

THE GUARDIAN SPIRIT
DULLY
JITTERWIT
VON GONKTOP
THE MASTER
CHIEF UGGLAMUGGLA
SAVAGES
THE OVERSEER
THE SAGE

Enter GUARDIAN SPIRIT.

GUARDIAN SPIRIT: I am a guardian spirit.

> Never mind whose.
>
> I am here to show you a strange happening.
>
> Whether you believe it or not
>
> Does not matter
>
> Because it is quite true, and doesn't need your belief
>
> To help it.
>
> Here is a scene with trees, an inn, and a road.
>
> Dawn is just opening.
>
> A man comes round the side of the inn
>
> And sits on a bench, under the window.
>
> He is carrying heavy bags.
>
> He has been sleeping in an outhouse.
>
> He cannot see me, for he is a human being.
>
> He speaks.

DULLY *has entered, carrying two big kitbags. He sits, yawns, gazes blissfully into the distance. Birdsong – dawn chorus.*

DULLY: Dawn – must be God's own favourite hour of the twenty-four.

> I think so. And the birds seem to think so – they're bubbling over.
>
> Everything's glittering.
>
> Back at home, the cocks will be stepping in through the just-opened doorway.
>
> The donkeys will be winding themselves up for the day, cranking their voices.
>
> The cows will be making a broad dark track through the dew
>
> Over the silver meadows

[29]

Coming to be milked.
And the mountains, the mountains blue beyond
   mountains,
Like old drunken sages,
They'll be stretched out in the dew, hazing and
   sipping.
And my dad, he'll be singing:
'In good King Charles's golden days
When loyalty no harm meant . . . '
Enter JITTERWIT *in a feverish hurry.*

JITTERWIT: Where's the Master? What's going on? Don't
   just sit.
   Get everything ready. Isn't he here?
   I've had a terrible night, a terrible night!
   I want to ask him a vital question. I've got to ask him.
   I can't bear it another minute.

DULLY: He's not here yet. What's the matter?

JITTERWIT: I can't bear it. It's terrible!

DULLY: What is?

JITTERWIT: It! It! Oh oaf! When are you going to wake up
   to it?

DULLY: If you don't sleep you get sick.

JITTERWIT: Where's Von Gonktop with the telescope?
   Enter VON GONKTOP *with an enormous telescope.*

VON GONKTOP: Where's the Master? Isn't he here yet? No?
   Are you ready? Is everything ready? Come on, snap to it.
   We can't play about, we're racing against time.

DULLY: I'm always ready, Mr Von Gonktop.

VON GONKTOP: His great brain's probably got him tied up
   in some problem. We must be patient. We're lucky
   he's as patient with us as he is. We're lucky he's
   taking us with him, do you know that? We're lucky to
   be sharing the honours.

[30]

JITTERWIT: Aren't we going to look through the telescope this morning?

VON GONKTOP: I've already looked.

JITTERWIT: Well?

VON GONKTOP: Worse than ever. Closer than ever. Huger than ever. Now it has a big blue spiky ring round it, like a gigantic flying gas-ring.

JITTERWIT: A blue ring! That wasn't there yesterday.

VON GONKTOP: Yesterday it wasn't as close, was it?
It's travelling at thousands of miles a second
Straight towards us, so it grows.
Closer and closer and closer.
Soon it will be here, it will arrive –
And Bang! – Whooooof!

JITTERWIT: What shall we do? What shall we do? Let me look.

JITTERWIT *looks through the telescope, up into the sky.*

Enter the MASTER – *a bearded scientist.*

MASTER: Well, and how is my little meteor this morning?

JITTERWIT: I can't bear to look. It'll turn my hair white!
Master, isn't there any chance . . .

MASTER: Bags packed? Are we ready?

JITTERWIT: Master, can I ask a question?

MASTER: Hurry up, we ought to be off.

JITTERWIT: Can't this meteor possibly miss us? I know it can't, I know your calculations are infallible, but – can't it possibly, just by a hairsbreadth, miss us?

MASTER: Gentlemen, the laws of the Universe are our laws.
If a meteor is hurtling out of the depths of space,
A colossal moon of flying metal
In a dazzlingly beautiful blue halo of fire,
Aimed directly at our insignificant earth,

Why, gentlemen, we simply have to accept it.
The Truth is the Truth.

VON GONKTOP: The Truth Is The Truth.

JITTERWIT: Yes, of course. And you know I've given up
everything for the Truth. My home, my job, my friends,
my happiness . . .

VON GONKTOP: The Master's calculations cannot fail.

MASTER: Out of the question.

VON GONKTOP: The Master has calculated the meteor will
arrive within a few days.

JITTERWIT: Aaaaah!

VON GONKTOP: The Master has calculated that it will shatter
the whole earth and everything on it, within a single
second, into red-hot dust.

JITTERWIT: Aaaaah!

VON GONKTOP: The Master has calculated the exact point of
its first contact with the earth, and we shall be there, to
receive it, if we hurry.

JITTERWIT: The exact point!

MASTER: We are going to stare up into it, unafraid, objective
to the last, observant to the last, scientific to the last, with
our filter-cameras aligned, as it comes smashing down on
to our heads. To the last, we shall be gazing up into the
blazing body of the Truth, as it comes smashing down on
our heads.

JITTERWIT: No!

VON GONKTOP: We are going to face the Truth.

MASTER: We must accept the Truth.

JITTERWIT: Help! We're finished!

    DULLY *falls off his bench. He lies snoring.*

MASTER: We are citizens of the Universe.

VON GONKTOP: We are citizens of the Universe.

MASTER: We accept the Universe. Repeat that.

VON GONKTOP *and* JITTERWIT: We accept the
    Universe.
MASTER (*to* DULLY): Wake up. We're off.
DULLY: Hmm?
MASTER: Wake up.
DULLY: Eh? What? Where? Oh!
VON GONKTOP: We're off to meet the Truth. You're our
    porter, so move.
JITTERWIT: The Master is leading us to the Truth. We will
    follow him to the end.
MASTER: We are noble mankind. Let us not forget it.
JITTERWIT: The Truth! The Truth!
VON GONKTOP: We want the whole Truth.
MASTER: The Absolute Truth.
JITTERWIT: And nothing but the Truth – no, nothing. Yes,
    yes, yes.
    Exeunt these three, shouting these slogans.
DULLY: That's the way they carry on all the time
    While I lug their belongings.
    They gas about renovating the whole globe
    While I cook their grub.
    They're wailing about the horrible Nothingness of Outer
        Space
    While I mend their boots.
    If you ask me, they're all brains and no sense.
    Still, as they say, I'm only an oaf.
    Only an oaf, only an oaf,
    And I've only got my loaf
    To think with.
    Re-enter VON GONKTOP, *furious.*
VON GONKTOP: There you are! Idiot! You're holding us
    back. March!
    Exeunt.

GUARDIAN SPIRIT: That is how it begins. And now see what
    follows.
    They travel over mountains, through cities, over seas
    Towards their meeting with the Truth.
    And the whole way the Master spreads his wisdom.
    His two disciples wonder if he is a god
    Walking the earth
    He can work such miracles, so calmly,
    Under the doom of the oncoming meteor
    Which, every day,
    They study carefully through their telescope.
MASTER: It's a pity it's only visible during the day.
    It's probably a fragment of the sun.
    But what a dazzling show it would make in the darkness.
VON GONKTOP: It is definitely getting bigger.
    Now there's a red ring, a hideous inflammation,
    Surrounding the blue ring.
JITTERWIT: I have said goodbye to everything.
    Goodbye to the trees, goodbye to the stones, the water,
    Goodbye to the . . .
MASTER: March! There's still two hundred miles to go.
GUARDIAN SPIRIT: They travel over the desert, through bad
    lands, and through swamps.
    Everywhere the Master spreads his wisdom.
    How does he spread his wisdom?
    And what is his wisdom?
    You shall see his wisdom.
    At last they come to the jungle of red flowers.
    Here, where their meteor is to fall,
    They discover the half-people, who are covered with
    brown fur.
    Wild drumming and singing.
MASTER: At last! The spot! This is the very spot

Where the meteor will first touch our earth,
According to my calculations.

VON GONKTOP: Which are infallible.

MASTER: Nothing could be better.

JITTERWIT: Is this where we're going to be smashed to bits?

MASTER: Set down the bags. Pitch the tents. Gather wood,
    find water.
    Get the cooker going.
    This is the exact spot.
    The dead centre of the meteor is aiming precisely there,
    There, where that red flower is, about there.
    On this spot
    We shall all disappear into the dead centre of the final
      Truth
    Smashed to blazing atoms.

VON GONKTOP: The Final Truth!
    (JITTERWIT *is sobbing.*)
    What's the matter, Jitterwit?

JITTERWIT: I can't bear it.

MASTER: Can't bear what?

JITTERWIT: It's so terrible – everything to go bang!
    Whooosh! Nothing. Not even gravestones.

MASTER: Why, man, even when you drop off in a doze
    it's as bad. Everything finishes.

JITTERWIT: Yes, but then I wake up.

MASTER: And here too you'll wake up. You'll wake up as
    cosmic fire. You'll have been sucked up into the Universe
    like a spoonful of medicine.
    What's all that racket?

DULLY: Savages, sir.

MASTER: Savages?

DULLY: They're having a jamboree. They're roasting a
    hippopotamus.

[35]

MASTER: It's impossible.

DULLY: What is?

MASTER: There are no savages left. Progress has cleaned up the whole globe. This is the year A.D. 2000. What do they think they're up to?

DULLY: They're savages, sir.

VON GONKTOP: Here, in this tangled jungle, they've been overlooked.

DULLY: They're very special savages, sir.

MASTER: Special? How special?

DULLY: Well, sir, they're covered with brown hair and they have little stumpy tails.

MASTER: Gorillas! Heavens, I've discovered a civilization of gorillas. Gorillas dancing and singing! The gorillas are evolving!

DULLY: No, sir. Not gorillas, people.

MASTER: Well, let's have a closer look at them.
And even though this globe's doomed within days,
Can we let these people carry on in their ignorance?

VON GONKTOP: No. Definitely not.

MASTER: Can we leave them in the misery of their poverty, their diseases, their wretched housing, their appalling diet?

VON GONKTOP: Definitely not.

MASTER: We stand for the advance and happiness of all mankind equally, not excluding even gorillas.

VON GONKTOP: We stand for the advance and happiness of all mankind equally, not excluding even gorillas.

MASTER: Where's my pistol?
(*Fires two shots. Singing and dancing stop.*)
That'll bring them over. Hellooooo!
Remember, tell them nothing about the meteor.
It might make them lose hope before we've had a chance to improve them.

[36]

Here they are.

JITTERWIT: Just as you said.

MASTER: Heavens, look at them. They're half-monkeys.
    They're covered with brown hair. And look at those
        funny little tails.
    What a discovery.

CHIEF: White men!

MASTER: They speak.

CHIEF: Friends!

MASTER: And they're friendly. Now these simple people shall
    have my help.

GUARDIAN SPIRIT: The Master begins to help the savages.
    First, he clears away the forest, burns it to the ground,
    So there'll be room for vast crops.
    Second, he shoots, poisons and traps all the wild
        beasts
    That might be a danger, with their long fangs and their
        hunger.
    Third, he destroys all the wild creatures
    That might eat the crops.
    Fourth, he poisons all the insects
    That would infect the crops with their invisible eggs.
    Fifth, he poisons all green growth that is not crops,
    That might stifle the crops.
    And now as far as a man can walk in a day
    Like a sea the wheat flows under the wind
    Towards the horizon.

MASTER: Meanwhile through space
    Every second thousands of miles closer
    The meteor rushes with its blazing mouth
    To swallow the earth.

    JITTERWIT *and* VON GONKTOP, *with telescope.*

VON GONKTOP: Are you still afraid?

[37]

JITTERWIT: I've got past being afraid, I think.
I think.
The Master's confidence is a great support.
Yes, I accept the end of everything
If it means the Truth.

VON GONKTOP: The smash should be tremendous.
It will be visible all over the galaxy, probably.
Of course, we shan't see it. We shall be it.

JITTERWIT: How many days now?

VON GONKTOP: A few. The master is working it out
exactly. That's what he's busy at.

JITTERWIT: Great is the Master!

VON GONKTOP: Nothing turns the Master from the
Truth.

JITTERWIT: He respects nothing, neither man, woman,
nor child, but the Truth.

VON GONKTOP: Nothing has any truth for him but the
Truth.

JITTERWIT: What is the Truth?

VON GONKTOP: There. That is the Truth. Blazing down
towards the earth.

JITTERWIT: Oh, I daren't look. I daren't look any more.

VON GONKTOP: But you must. You must stare the Truth in
the face.

JITTERWIT *looks.*

JITTERWIT: Now there's a purple ring round the red ring.
A blue ring, a red ring, a purple ring
Like a terrific target.
We're the target! I can't look.
Enter CHIEF *of savages.*

CHIEF: Hail!

VON GONKTOP: Ah, Chief Ugglamuggla, what's the news?

CHIEF: Where is the Master?

VON GONKTOP: What's the matter? You're in a sweat.

CHIEF: Where is the Master?

VON GONKTOP: Please don't look so fierce. He's in his tent.
    But don't disturb him, he's deep in calculation.

CHIEF: I must speak with the Master, quick.

VON GONKTOP: Come back. Don't disturb him.
    He is calculating the date of the arrival of the Truth.

CHIEF: Our wheat is on fire. All the horizons are blazing.
    All our food has gone up in smoke. Master!
    All run out.

DULLY: Now the entire landscape is black ashes.
    The savages have no more food,
    Except what they'd dried and preserved from the earlier
        days
    When it grew on the trees.
    There is no jungle fruit now, the Master cleared all the
        jungle.
    There are no game animals, he poisoned them all.
    There is nothing on the plains but a hot wind
    Carrying ashes.
    But the Master has a solution.
    He sends for machines.
    The savages will make motor-cars.
    He has them building factories, to make motor-cars.
    The savages will send their motor-cars abroad,
    And in payment they will get food back.
    The savages set to work, because they are hungry.
    If you ask me, this is a great disaster
    For these savages. Here they come
    Carrying spades to dig foundations
    Of the factories.
    SAVAGES *go over the stage, carrying spades.* OVERSEER
    goads them on.

OVERSEER: Get along there. Sweat. Work. If you don't want
   to starve
   Get moving. The factories have to be built.
   They're our one chance. Factories have to be built
   To build the motor-cars to buy the bread.
   Get a move on.

FIRST SAVAGE: When will the bread be here? Our families
   are hungry.

SECOND SAVAGE: Our chief has grown cruel.
   He drives us to dig foundations.
   When we tire, he beats us.

OVERSEER: Fools, if you don't dig there'll be no bread.
   Both you and he will starve. And me, too. Move.

DULLY: Now the motor-cars are driving
   Off the production line.
   The Master has made everything go like magic
   With his great brain.
   Now the first consignment of motor-cars
   Drives away, to be loaded on to ships, at the port.
   Soon, says the Master, soon now bread will be
      coming
   With other tasty titbits.

ALL: Bread, bread, we want bread.
   We've built the motor-cars, where is the bread?

ONE SAVAGE: Where are the hippos and the paw-paw
   fruit?

ALL: Bread, bread, we want bread.
   We've built the motor-cars, where is the bread?

TWO SAVAGES: Our families are starving.
   Wailing of the families.

ALL: Our families are starving.

DULLY: Now they refuse to build more motor-cars
   Till they get bread. They down tools.

OVERSEER: Work. Work. Work.

ALL: Bread. Bread. Bread. Bread. Bread. Bread. We want bread.

This goes on in background.

CHIEF: Listen to my people.

MASTER: Their distress is understandable.
Tell them bread is coming, shiploads of it.
To pay for the lovely motor-cars they built.
But they must not stop building motor-cars
To buy yet more bread after that bread's finished.
When they stop building motor-cars, they starve.
Tell them that.

CHIEF: I will tell them.

CHIEF *goes.*

MASTER: These wretched savages certainly are unlucky.
Who would have thought their wheatfields would catch fire,
Leaving them foodless. Yet what does it matter?
In exactly an hour, the meteor arrives,
Lands on our skulls and smashes the globe to bits.
That will solve their problems, thank goodness.
I have calculated the exact second.
I'll go and prepare the cameras.

Exit, as JITTERWIT *wanders in.*

JITTERWIT: Did you hear that? In an hour.

DULLY: What's the matter, Mr Jitterwit?

JITTERWIT: We're finished! One more hour and everything's finished.

DULLY: Don't you take it so hard.

JITTERWIT: The Master has made his calculations, it's all tied up.

DULLY: Don't you take it to heart.

JITTERWIT: Oaf! You don't understand!

[41]

DULLY: Well, I know I'm an oaf, but your master seems a bit
    stupid to me, making all this fuss.

JITTERWIT: Stupid? Do you know what you're saying?
    He's the most famous man on earth at the moment.

DULLY: But all this rubbish about a meteor!

JITTERWIT: But that's exactly it. You could almost call it his
    meteor.
    He's calculated the speed, the weight,
    The exact point and moment
    At which it will strike. And it's right here, in an hour.

DULLY: Don't get worked up.

JITTERWIT: I don't want to die. I don't want the world
    To be blasted to bits. I like it.
    Why shouldn't I get worked up?

DULLY: Well, I can't see this meteor.

JITTERWIT: Have you looked through the telescope?
    It's a blazing golden ball
    With a fierce blue circle around it
    And around that circle, a fierce red bigger circle,
    And around that one, a fierce purple circle –
    It's rushing to swallow us up, bigger every minute.

DULLY: Show me.

JITTERWIT: Look, imbecile, look.

DULLY: Ah, yes.

JITTERWIT: Ah yes, he says. Aren't you scared out of your
    wits?
    What are you doing? What are you doing?
    Unscrewing the telescope?

DULLY: Well, look. There's your meteor
    Inside the telescope.

JITTERWIT: Aaaaaah!

DULLY: It's a spot of fungus growing on the lens.
    A spot of lurid mould. You see, yellow centre,

Then a blue ring, then a red, then a purple –
It must be growing quite fast in this climate.
JITTERWIT: Ooooh! It's a blot of penicillin!
Our meteor's nothing but a spot of fungus!
The Master's been deceived by a mushroom!
Enter at great speed VON GONKTOP.
VON GONKTOP: Pack the bags. Strike camp. Run for your
lives.
A messenger has just arrived.
The whole shipload of motor-cars
Was sunk at sea by commercial pirates. The savages are
rising.
Wild drumming and yelling, off.
Enter the MASTER *at great speed.*
MASTER: Was it my fault? Can I control the seas?
They'd have become rich. They'd have become
A flourishing modern industrial society
Within a few years. They've done everything wrong.
They have no patience. They cannot listen to sense.
Civilization has taught them nothing.
Now their cars are sunk at sea and all their land is
ruined.
Run, drop everything and run.
They're going to eat us. They're suddenly cannibals.
There's nothing left for them but to eat us.
All run off. Drums and wild yells louder.

GUARDIAN SPIRIT: The Master and his disciples and the
porter
Run for their lives
Across the blackened plains. They escape
Back to civilization.

They have cleaned the telescope.
And though they can no longer see any meteor
Their confidence is restored,
For now the lens is clean.

MASTER: We shall not make the same mistake again.

VON GONKTOP: And we reacted to what we thought was the
world's end
In the very noblest way. We marched to meet it.

JITTERWIT: We are proud of ourselves.

MASTER: We acted sensibly and very nobly
And, to the last, like true scientists.
We pursued what we thought was the Truth, and nothing
stopped us, nothing.
Only our thoughts were mistaken,
For we are merely men.

VON GONKTOP: And man is full of error.

MASTER: Man is himself an error.
Only the Truth can make man greater than man,
Can make him the Truth.

DULLY: And so we wandered the world.
And everywhere we went
The Master spread his wisdom.
And everywhere he spread his wisdom
The lands blackened, the wind blew hot with ashes,
And men were plunged in discontent,
Misery and deprivation.
And motor-car factories arose to make them happy.
Did the motor-car factories make men happy?
Or if not motor-car factories, canning factories.
Did canning factories make men happy?
Or if not canning factories,
Mental hospitals,
And beside the mental hospitals,

Hospitals.
And beside the hospitals,
Crematoria.

But there was one thing the Master could not do.
He could not make the dead live.
He could not turn the dead into the living.
Nor where he had created a desolation
Could he create grass.

MASTER: What good is all my wisdom?
  What good is all my mastery of the laws
  Of creation? I cannot create life.

DULLY: The problem kept him awake.
  He beat his brains on his books, on his formulae.
  And at last he thought he almost had it.
  And at that moment he heard of a wise man
  Who lived on a remote mountain
  Who could revive the dead. He could make the dead live
  So ran the rumour,
  And out of the dead stone he could bring grass.

MASTER: A man wiser than I am? Impossible!
  Let him test his knowledge against mine.
  He can revive the dead? Impossible!
  So could I, if I were really put to the test.
  Let him test his wisdom against mine.
  We'll expose this faker.

VON GONKTOP: No man is wiser than the Master.
  No man has greater knowledge
  Of the mysteries of creation
  Than the Master.

JITTERWIT: Praise him! Praise him!

VON GONKTOP: You could make the dead live, if you really
    tried.

You have not really tried.

MASTER: Yes, I believe I could.

VON GONKTOP: You have never truly tested yourself.

MASTER: Eureka!

JITTERWIT: What? What is it?

MASTER: I can raise the dead. I say I can.

(*Both cheer.*)

I will test my powers against this man.

DULLY: Once more we grew blisters inside our boots,
Stumbling over the wastelands of this world.
We came to the mountains, the blue tepees of the gods.
I am a simple man, I believe in gods.
We climbed, where wild goats leaned out
Over gulfs full of the whisper of torrents
And gunfire of landslides. We climbed
Where eagles slid from us and hung out
Over a five-mile drop into forest.
We climbed. We climbed till our brains altered
And we could see mountains upside down
On top of the mountains. We saw smoke like horsehair
   stuffing
Belching out of a crevice between stones.
When we got closer, there was no smoke. Nothing
But a solitary blue mountain flower, the size of a shirt-
   button.
Then we heard a tremendous klaxon voice announcing
   the winner
That suddenly stopped. Later, a woman's head sank from
   the air
Floating between us, waist-high, smiling at us,
And gliding on down the mountain. We climbed
Till we came to a cave.
I can tell you, it was hard going. In front of the cave

An ancient man was sitting, watching us climb.
The hair and beard of a goat, and decorated
With feathers and talons of eagles.

MASTER: Good day, sir. I said, Good day, sir.

VON GONKTOP: He doesn't seem to see or hear
Even though we've got so near.

MASTER: I said: Good day, sir.

SAGE: So you've come.

MASTER: Of course I've come. Why, did you expect me?

SAGE: Of course I expected you.

MASTER: Hm! How? Rumours, I suppose.

SAGE: You are the first human beings
To have trod this slope.

MASTER: Ha-hah. Then you must know why I've come, if
you're a thought-reader.

SAGE: Of course.

MASTER: Hmm!

VON GONKTOP: Watch him, Master, he's going to pull a fast
one.

JITTERWIT: If he pulls a fast one, it will be his last one.

MASTER: This is Von Gonktop, Research Assistant.

SAGE: Greetings.

MASTER: This is Mr Jitterwit, Laboratory Attendant.

SAGE: Greetings. And what is the name of your leader?

MASTER: Me. I'm the leader. The whole world knows me as
the Master.
I have given up my private name.

SAGE: But who is that fourth one, your leader?

VON GONKTOP: Look out, I think he's needling us.

JITTERWIT: The ugly, scruffy, whiskery cuss!

MASTER: The fourth? There are only three of us.

SAGE: I see four.

MASTER: O, him. He's only the porter. He's just the man.

SAGE: So he is your leader!

MASTER: He is not! I am! Impudence!

SAGE: Greetings and blessings, wise one.

DULLY: Who, me? I thank you, sir. And a good day to you,
     sir, too.

MASTER: Impudence!

VON GONKTOP: Look at the rascal's dirty dhoti.

JITTERWIT: He's certainly lousy and probably potty.

MASTER: Wait a minute. Do you know who I am?

SAGE: Of course.

MASTER: You know what I've done?

SAGE: Of course.

MASTER: You know I am called the Wisest Man In The
     World.

SAGE: And I know the Dog is called the dog
     And I know the Mud is called the mud.

VON GONKTOP: Did you hear what he said?

JITTERWIT: Crack him over the head.

MASTER: Sir, I suspect you are mocking me.

SAGE: Then come to the point.

MASTER: I challenge you to a test of mental strength.
     Do you accept or don't you? If you don't
     Then I take it I've won.

SAGE: You see those bones scattered among the rocks?

MASTER: Those are the bones of a tiger.
     An unusually large specimen.

SAGE: Correct.
     I can assemble the bones of that tiger
     With a single word.

MASTER: With only a word? But that's absurd.

SAGE: Agagagagagagaga!

MASTER: Haha! So much for that. Nothing.

SAGE: Agagagagagagagaga!

JITTERWIT: They moved!

SAGE: Agagagagagagagagagagagagagagagagagagagaga

As he goes on, the others say

JITTERWIT: They're moving.

VON GONKTOP: It's astounding. They're bounding together
like rats and mice.

MASTER: Hmmm!

VON GONKTOP: He's done it.

SAGE *is silent.*

MASTER: A very crafty trick!

A perfectly assembled skeleton. Congratulations.

I suppose, though, that's the limit of your powers?

SAGE: I can put flesh and blood and skin on to the bones
With a single word.

MASTER: I'd like to see that! That I cannot believe!

JITTERWIT: He's pretty slick!

VON GONKTOP: It's just a trick.

SAGE: I drape my tiger skin over the skeleton: so.

MASTER: Well, go ahead.

SAGE: Gohogogogogogogogogogogogogogogogogogogogog!

MASTER: Nothing yet, is there?

SAGE: Gohogogogogogogogogogogogogogogogogog!

JITTERWIT: It moved. I saw it. It moved.

SAGE: Gohogogogogogogogogogogogogogogogogogogogo-
gogogogogog

He goes on.

DULLY: Look out, Master, look out.

VON GONKTOP: A tiger! A tiger!

MASTER: Heavens! My word and goodness gracious!

He's actually done it. Dear me, dear me.

This is going to be difficult, I can see.

(SAGE *is now silent.*)

But is this tiger dead or living?

DULLY: If it's living, let's be leaving.

SAGE: Alas, this glorious tiger, perfect as it is
In every anatomical detail, is dead.

MASTER: So then your powers are not such a great wonder.
It was mainly bragging and propaganda.
You've no real thunderbolts, you've just got thunder.

SAGE: Alas, there are limits to my powers.

MASTER: But I heard you could revive the dead
And set them jumping for meat and bread.

SAGE: Untrue.

MASTER: Well, I can. I can revive the dead.
I will bring life back into this tiger.
Porter, pass the bag of instruments.

DULLY: Master, be careful.

MASTER: Pass it. The hypodermic syringe.

DULLY: But, Master, this is a tiger – if you can revive it –

VON GONKTOP: Praise the Master's wisdom, he can revive
the dead.

JITTERWIT: He can set them howling for meat and bread.

VON GONKTOP: He can set them leaping higher than your
head.

BOTH: Praise him! Praise him! Praise him!
We have given our lives into the keeping of his wisdom.

MASTER: We call this little magic wand a hypodermic syringe.
I shall just jab this needle into the tiger –

DULLY: Wait, wait.

MASTER: What?

DULLY: Please just give me time to squeeze myself
Into the top of that solitary, straggly thorn tree.

MASTER: What, are you afraid?

VON GONKTOP: Coward!

JITTERWIT: Coward!

VON GONKTOP: Run from progress.

JITTERWIT: Run in fear from the mighty achievements of
    man.

DULLY: Yes, oh yes, I'm a coward when it comes to tigers
    That haven't had a bite for many a year.
    Exit DULLY.

MASTER: Behold, I stick this needle into the tiger.

DULLY (*off*): Goodbye.

MASTER: And I inject. Rise, tiger, awake:
    Lift up thy body and walk.
    (*Terrific roar of a tiger.*)
    I've done it! I've done it!

JITTERWIT *and* VON GONKTOP: Hip, hip, hooray.
    Hip, hip, hoor – AAAAAAAAAAAAAaaaaaaaaaaahhhh!
    All scream. Horrible roar.
    Roar upon roar. Their screams die.
    Long silence.

DULLY: The tiger ate them all.
    The tiger ate the Master, hair and fingernails and all.
    The tiger ate them all.
    The tiger ate Von Gonktop from his big toe to his
       eyeball.
    The tiger ate them all.
    The tiger ate poor Jitterwit, and it ground his bones up
       small.
    The tiger ate them all.

    But isn't it strange?
    The moment the tiger jumped to its feet
    The whiskery old man vanished – just disappeared.
    Pop – gone, like a bubble.
    And there was only a tiger, swallowing my comrades.
    So now I'm going home, none the wiser.
    I'll have to think of a moral to this story.

GUARDIAN SPIRIT: So the porter returns to his father's farm.
    Where the cockerels shake their metals
    And the donkeys crank their voices
    And the cows sway, heavier than tubs of butter,
    And the mountains say nothing
    But stay as they are, stretched full length in the sun,
    Smoking idly, gazing up into the blue.
    And the farmer, strolling around his boundary, sings:
DULLY: In good King Charles's golden days
    When loyalty no harm meant . . .

BEAUTY AND THE BEAST

CHARACTERS

THE FLOORSWEEPER
THE FATHER
HIS SON
HIS DAUGHTER FLOREAT
THE DOCTOR
THE BEARKEEPER
THE BEAR

Enter FLOORSWEEPER.

FLOORSWEEPER: I don't know what's going on in this house,
    I don't.
    It's all very funny. And not very nice.
    The master is a millionaire
    But that doesn't help him.
    Something's mysteriously wrong with his daughter.
    Something's wrong with his daughter and he dotes on
    her.
    What good are his millions, his yachts, his Rolls,
    His thousands of acres crawling with leopards and
    peacocks,
    None of it can help her.
    She just gets paler and paler.
    He can't sign a cheque to put some colour in her cheeks.
    But what's wrong with his daughter?

Enter FATHER *and* SON.

FATHER: This is the eighth doctor.

SON: He's probably no good either.

FATHER: Was she screaming last night?

SON: She woke me three times, father.

FATHER: Do you know what I'm suspecting?

SON: Don't tell me you think it's witchcraft.

FATHER: Witchcraft. Yes, witchcraft.

SON: Witchcraft doesn't exist.

FATHER: Doctors peer under her eyelids, finger her pulses,
    Listen to her lungs, study her blood,
    Diet her on parsley, then on salami,
    Then make her fast on water. They're useless.
    There's nothing wrong with her body.
    It's all in her mind. She's bewitched.

[55]

SON: It's beyond me, anyway.

FATHER: The doctor's whispering in there with her.

SON: That'll be another bill as long as a dog-chain
    With some dreadful figure snarling at the end of it.

FATHER: Money! Money! Why, money's nothing
    If they can cure her. If they could make her smile.
    She's just lost interest in everything.
    If they could make her smile, that would be something.

SON: Maybe a laugh would jerk her out of it.

FATHER: Maybe you're right. Maybe a laugh would do it.
    (*Enter* DOCTOR, *leading the daughter*, FLOREAT.)
    Here she is. Now, how are you this morning?

DOCTOR: Shhhh! Keep off. Don't disturb her.
    What are all these people crowding here for?

FATHER: These are my family, my servants, my men –
    They love my daughter, they've come to show their
        concern.

DOCTOR: She must be left alone. Kept quiet.
    Given soft music. She must not be crowded and stared
        at.

SON: Nonsense. Come on, let's make her laugh.
    All she needs is some merriment.
    Hahahahahahaha!
    All laugh, prolonged laughter. FLOREAT *grows sadder.*

DOCTOR: Stop! Stop! STOP!
    (*Laughter dies.*)
    You'll send her crazy. Are you crazy?

SON: Well, it didn't help much, for sure, did it?

DOCTOR: Now all of you leave.

FATHER: Wait. Now, Floreat, my little mouse,
    What do you want? Shall we go yachting?
    (*She shakes her head.*)
    Fishing for bonito, in the Gulf of Mexico?

[56]

(*She shakes her head.*)

Shall we go hunting gazelles, in Arabia, with cheetahs?

(*She shakes her head.*)

How about some gliding in the Alps?

(*She shakes her head.*)

How about some gambling? Blow in a million.

That should get your circulation going.

(*She shakes her head.*)

How about a tour through Baluchistan?

You could get some carpets for your room.

FLOREAT: Nothing! I don't want anything. Leave me
 alone.

DOCTOR: You see? Now, if you please, all of you, leave.

FATHER: You know the reward, Doctor, if you cure her.

SON: What she needs is entertainment

 Of a surprising sort. Something lively.

FATHER: Everybody out.

 All exeunt, except DOCTOR *and* FLOREAT.

DOCTOR: Now, my girl, tell me just what's wrong.

 Describe it to me.

FLOREAT: It's horrible.

DOCTOR: Describe it. I can't cure it till you describe it.

FLOREAT: It's too horrible.

DOCTOR: Nothing's that horrible. Now, it comes over you
 after dark. Is that right?

FLOREAT: Yes.

DOCTOR: While you're asleep?

FLOREAT: Yes.

DOCTOR: And what does it look like? Hm?

FLOREAT: I daren't think.

DOCTOR: Well, is it – er – a ghost?

FLOREAT: No, not quite.

DOCTOR: Not quite! Is it a bird?

FLOREAT: No.

DOCTOR: Do you see it?

FLOREAT: No.

DOCTOR: Hm! Do you hear it?

FLOREAT: Yes.

DOCTOR: And what sound does it make?

FLOREAT: No!

DOCTOR: No what?

FLOREAT (*screams*): I can't bear to think of it.

    She begins to wail and cry. Enter FATHER.

FATHER: What's going on? What are you doing to her?

DOCTOR: Shhh! Will you please leave us alone.

    I was just getting to it.

FATHER: Have a care, Doctor. Nothing too drastic.

    Her nerves are not too strong.

DOCTOR: Yes, well, I think she'd better rest.

    I think she'd better go back to bed for a while.

    She's missing her sleep. Perhaps she could snatch some sleep,

    While I'm thinking of a cure.

FATHER: Back to bed, Floreat. Get some sleep.

    (*Exit* FLOREAT.)

    Well, what have you discovered?

DOCTOR: Nothing – except there's something.

FATHER: We knew that. We don't need to finance a doctor

    To be told that. I can tell you more.

    It's something so hideous no woman

    Will stay the night with her. They come out screaming.

    But they don't know what's frightened them either.

DOCTOR: Hm! Most mysterious!

FATHER: Is it a demon? Is she haunted by a demon

    Like Sarah, in the book of Tobit?

    A terrible, man-killing demon? Or what?

DOCTOR: I have an idea.

FATHER: We need one.

DOCTOR: Tonight, I'll hide under her bed.

FATHER: Hm!

DOCTOR: If it's something outside her own brain –
Why, I shall see it. Or hear it.
I shall feel it anyway. I shall have met it.
I doubt if it will drive me out screaming.
Maybe then I can treat it.

FATHER: Good. I like it. Do it. Tonight.

DOCTOR: Tonight it is.

Exeunt. Enter FLOORSWEEPER.

FLOORSWEEPER: I don't like the looks of this at all.
The poor girl gets whiter and whiter.
Her eyes are droopy weepy
Or else dry and staring.
And this doctor's an idiot.
All doctors are a sort of idiot, if you ask me.
They're so smart, they become idiots.
Now he's hiding under her bed
To catch her ailment red-handed.
Every month it's a new one.
Well, she breaks my heart
To have such idiots gambolling around her
When she's so sick.

Exit. FLOREAT *climbs into bed. Enter* DOCTOR.

DOCTOR: There she lies on her bed. She falls asleep readily
To say she has such nightmares waiting for her.
If I creep out of sight here under her bed . . .
(*He creeps under the bed.*)
Now, whatever it is, coming to get her,
Let it come. I'm ready for it. Shhhhh! Listen.

FLOREAT (*softly*): Ooooooh!

[59]

DOCTOR: Is she asleep?

   He peers out.

FLOREAT (*louder*): Oooooooh!

DOCTOR: Something's coming. Something's here. What is it?

   Loud steady banging.

TREMENDOUS VOICE: Let me in. Let me in. I've come for
   you.

FLOREAT [*almost a cry*]: Ooooooh!

   *Bangings grow louder and more violent, seem to come
   first from one side then from the other, and the voice,
   louder and closer, seems likewise to come from all sides.*

VOICE: I've come for you. Awake and let me in.

   I'm coming to get you. Awake and open the doors.

   DOCTOR *jumps out.*

DOCTOR: Get away, whatever you are, get away, out of it!

   (*He bangs the fire-irons, etc., together.*)

   Help! Help! Help!

   FLOREAT *wakes, begins to scream.*

   Door bursts open, enter FATHER *and* SON *in nightshirts.*

FATHER: What's going on? Hello? Hello? Hello?

FLOREAT: Daddy!

FATHER: It's all right, my little love, it's me.

SON: What was it?

FATHER: Where is it?

SON: Did you see it?

DOCTOR: It's gone.

   Exeunt. Enter FLOORSWEEPER.

FLOORSWEEPER: Well, what was it? I just wonder.

   If you ask me, this place is fearfully haunted.

   It's a revenge from heaven, for her father being so rich,

   It's sinful to be so rich. It makes you stupid.

   And maybe this is his punishment.

   That frightened me last night, and I don't mind saying it.

Why, my hair stood on end, right up on end,
And I'm at the top of the house, in the attics.
The poor old dog must have heard it, he's still trembling.
He's jammed himself right back under the stove
And won't come out. He's still in there, whining.
The cats have disappeared, they've run off into the
    woods.
There are no sparrows in the yard. And all morning
I haven't seen a single cockroach or fly.
Everything's terrified and gone.
Everything's shunning this house.
Enter FATHER *and* DOCTOR.

FATHER: Tonight, I'll watch with you.

DOCTOR: Ah, it was horrible!

FATHER: So you keep saying. Describe it, exactly.

DOCTOR: It was – I can't quite say – it was –
    Horrible! Horrible!

FATHER: Hm! It seems to have been alarming all right.
    But it won't frighten me out of action.
    I shall bring along my pistols.
    I'm something of an expert, you know,
    At shooting trout through the head when they jump for
        flies,
    Or driving a nail in at fifty paces.

DOCTOR: I saw nothing to shoot at.

FATHER: Still shaken?

DOCTOR: My mouth tastes ghastly, like an old shoe.

FATHER: That's fear.

DOCTOR: I'll wait in her room with you, nevertheless.
    We must run this monster to earth.

FATHER: A monster, you call it.

DOCTOR: What else can we call it?

FATHER: How is she?

[61]

DOCTOR: Today she's bad. Lying in bed.
    She really hasn't the strength to move, not after last
        night.
FATHER: If we don't act tonight. I'm afraid
    We shall be too late.
DOCTOR: I am with you.
    FLOORSWEEPER *in her nightgown.*
FLOORSWEEPER: I'm not going to sleep tonight.
    I'm going to bed with a poker.
    The doctor and her father are fully armed.
    Her brother has been practising with his twelve-bore.
    The doctor and her father are under her bed.
    The brother is walking round and round the house.
    Eleven's already struck. There's no moon.
    Will it come tonight?
    There's not a breath of wind on the trees.
    Will it stir? Will it come? What's that?
    Enter SON.
SON: What are you doing here?
FLOORSWEEPER: Just going to bed, sir. It's a dark stair up to
        my room, sir,
    I was just screwing up courage.
    After last night, sir.
SON: Get up with you, it's nothing but my sister's nightmares.
FLOORSWEEPER: Oh, sir, you haven't seen the dog, how he's
        taken it.
SON: The dog?
FLOORSWEEPER: Or the cat.
SON: Why, what have they got to do with it?
FLOORSWEEPER: If I die of fright tonight, it won't be my
        fault.
SON: Silly old woman!
    SON *goes off whistling, she goes.*

DOCTOR *and* FATHER *peer from under* FLOREAT'*s bed.*

DOCTOR: Now's the time. Listen.

FATHER: There's not much room under this bed for
    manœuvres.

DOCTOR: Shhhhh!

    Twelve strikes.

FATHER: Not a sound. It's an unusually still night.

DOCTOR: Shhh!

FLOREAT (*muffled*): Oooooh! No! No!

FATHER: Is that Floreat? Floreat – are you all right?

DOCTOR: Shhhh! Let it come. Be still.

    Wind rises. Wind sounds increasing.

FATHER: The wind's getting up. Something's getting up.

DOCTOR: See that – lightning.

    Thunder.

TREMENDOUS VOICE: I have come for you.

FLOREAT: Help! Help!

    Thunder.

TREMENDOUS VOICE: I am coming in to get you! This time I
    shall get you!

DOCTOR: Here it comes again.

FATHER: It's an earthquake. This is an earthquake,
    The house is rocking.

TREMENDOUS VOICE: Now you will be mine.

    Thunder. FLOREAT *cries loud.*

DOCTOR: Look out. The wall's cracking open. It's an
    earthquake.

FATHER: There it is. Look. There. Look.

    (*He fires twice.*
    Thunder.
    Loud agonized wail goes off into the distance.
    Wind dies.
    Silence.)

[63]

I got him. I'm certain I got him.
Enter SON.

SON: What is it? Where is it?

FATHER: I got him. It's all right, my darling,
Your dad's here and I've killed the monster.

SON: What happened? I didn't see a thing.

FATHER: Where's the doctor?

SON: Here, under the bed.

FATHER: It's all right. You can come out. We've won.
Drag him out.

SON: Look at him, his hair's gone white.
It was black and it's gone snow-white.

FATHER: That's fear for you. That's real terror for you.

DOCTOR: Oh, I thought it was the end of the world.

FATHER: I saw a giant figure in the gap.
The walls were cracking open and this figure
Was tearing the crack wider and shoving in –
I fired twice, dead centre. I don't think I missed.
We're going to need the builders.

SON: No trace of him.

FATHER: Yes, there's blood, see it,
On the mirror, still dripping.

SON: And here's a spot of it on this powder compact.

FATHER: It's all right, Floreat, I got him.

SON: There's no body. He must have crawled away.

DOCTOR: Well, that settles one thing.

FATHER: What?

DOCTOR: It's not just in her mind, is it?

SON: And it's wounded.

FLOORSWEEPER: Three nights now and nothing's happened.
They say the monster has died in the forest.
Her father fired his pistol into its body.
But his daughter's no better.

If you ask me, she's worse.
But now the son's having a go, and they've sent the
    doctor packing.
He's glad to be going.
That night aged him ten years.
But now her brother's found her some amusement.
He's convinced that if she could laugh, she'd be cured.
So he's found her something amusing. Well, we'll see.
Enter SON.

SON: He's here. He's coming. Where's Floreat? Where is she?
    Here comes the bearkeeper. Here comes the Dancing
        Bear.
    What a bear!
    Black as the gullet of a chimney,
    With claws like garden forks,
    But he dances like a joker.
    Enter FATHER.

FATHER: Are you sure it's not a dangerous bear?
    Bears are notorious, they're shiftier than the weather.
    Every bear has two demons.
    One for plaguing himself, one for plaguing the world.
    When he strokes you, your arms fall off.
    Pipes. Enter BEARKEEPER *with* BEAR.

SON: What's wrong with your bear? What's that bandage?
    Has he been hurt?

BEARKEEPER: Good morning, good morning, ladies and
        gentlemen.
    First, I will explain this slight imperfection in my bear.
    A little accident, a teeny accident.
    An imbecile bird-hunter in the forest.
    My Bonzo – his majesty the bear
    Is called Bonzo – has a pet canary. Yes,
    He's so clever and tame, he keeps a canary.

[65]

Believe it or not. They are great friends,
Him and his pet canary.

FATHER: And what happened?

BEARKEEPER: Why, my Bonzo was playing with his pet.
He held up his paws, and the canary
Sat on his talon, pecking seeds from his lips.
We were sitting having our lunch in the forest.
The bird-hunter was creeping among the ferns.
He saw the bobbing yellow of the canary.
He did not see the burly black of Bonzo.
He thought Bonzo was the hairy bole of a yew tree
Where the canary was sitting. He fired. And he missed.
He hit my Bonzo's paw. Didn't he, Bonzo?

BONZO *roars*.

FATHER: Shouldn't you have him on a chain?

BEARKEEPER: Bonzo on a chain! Sacrilege!

SON: But maybe the wound's upset his temper a little.

BEARKEEPER: Look, I put my hand into his gullet.
And now – look. See him licking my throat?
Now – look – he hugs me. Love me, Bonzo.

SON: Look out, he'll squash you like a tube of toothpaste.

BEARKEEPER: No, no, no, he's very, very gentle.
See him licking my ear.

FATHER: That's amazing!

SON: Floreat, come and see the wonderful bear.

Enter FLOREAT.

FLOREAT: Oh, what a lovely beast!

FATHER: Ah, well. At least she likes something.
That's a start.

SON: Now make him dance and be comical.

BEARKEEPER: Stand back. Are you ready? Dance, Bonzo,
dance.

He pipes, the BEAR *dances*.

FATHER: Extraordinary! Amazing! Staggering! Stupendous!
SON: Look at Floreat, she's smiling.
  Piping stops.
FATHER: How much for your bear? I'll buy him.
BEARKEEPER: Sorry, sir, Bonzo could never leave me.
FATHER: I'll buy you both. How much for the two of you?
FLOREAT: Yes. Let me dance, I want to dance with the bear.
FATHER: Floreat, no.
FLOREAT: I want to, I want to, he can hold one end
  Of my ribbon and I'll hold the other.
BEARKEEPER: O he'll do that. He's very very clever,
  And very gentle.
SON: Let her, Father. Look at her. She's happy.
  Piping. BEAR *and* FLOREAT *dance.*
FATHER: Where's my camera? I must go get my camera.
  This is the shot of a lifetime.
  He runs out. BEAR *picks up* FLOREAT *and runs out.*
  FLOREAT *screams.*
SON: Stop! Stop! Father! The bear's got Floreat.
  The bear's running away with her.
  Come back. Fetch my guns, somebody.
  He's picked her up like a baby. He's snatched her.
  Help.
  He runs out. FATHER *runs in.*
FATHER: What? Which way? Which way did they go?
  Where've they gone? What's happened?
SON (*off*): This way. The bear's galloping into the forest,
  Over the fields and into the forest
  And Floreat's under his arm.
FATHER: It's the monster. The monster in the likeness of a
    bear!
  He's tricked us. The monster's got my daughter.
  Exeunt.

[67]

FLOORSWEEPER: Three days now that she's been gone
    Under the bear's arm. What is she by now?
    The bear would polish her off in a couple of hours.
    He'd crunch her bones on the second day.
    He'd chew her slippers and swallow them on the
      third.
    Bears eat everything.
    Her father is wild. He's combing the land with
      dogs.
    Her brother has sworn to skin it and nail the skin
    To the floor of the hallway, where all wipe their feet.
    But I think it's hopeless.
    The bear's devoured her by now, and gone away
    Over the mountain, to yawn in the next country.
    Bears are wise, even the horrible ones.
    All the hunters will come back with is sorrow.
    BEAR *and* FLOREAT *in cave.*
FLOREAT: Why are you keeping me in this cave?
    I've counted three nights. Why are you keeping me?
    Eat me and have done with it.
    (BEAR *growls.*)
    It's strange, but you seem to be a gentle bear.
    Was it really you who came at night
    Those other times? And did my father wound you?
    (BEAR *growls.*)
    You spoke then. Why can't you speak now?
    (BEAR *growls.*)
    Let me look at your bandage.
    But you look ferocious. Your eyes are the eyes
    That gloat into the smoking insides of a cow
    When you've torn it open.
    (BEAR *growls angrily.*)
    And your enormous talons. What are they for,

But for digging rabbits out of the earth,
Or the hearts out of men?
(BEAR *growls angrily*.)
And why are you so black? And so huge!
You are so prodigiously ugly!
If you are going to eat me eat me quickly.
(*She begins to sob.* BEAR *growls*.)
What are these? Bilberries again?
Have you brought me bilberries again?
And blackberries? And raspberries?
And wild watercress? And apples?
You're a mysteriously kind bear.
(BEAR *growls angrily*.)
What? What's the matter?
(*Yelping of hounds*.)
Hounds! The hunters! The hunters are coming.
They must have found your track.
It must be my father and the hunters.
(BEAR *growls*.)
Come back. They'll kill you. They'll kill you. Oh he's
gone.
They'll kill him if they see him.
(*Hounds now yelping close*.)
Why has he brought me here?
Why is he so kind to me?
Does he think I'm a bear?
For three days now he's fed me,
And watched me, and not once
Frightened me. Why? Why?
Why didn't he devour me?
Why did he bother to bring me?
Is he lonely here?
Now they're going to kill him.

To free me, they will kill him.
They will kill my bear.
I must stop them. Come back.
Gunshots. BEAR *roars. Hounds yelp.*

FATHER: I got him! I got him!
Enter the BEAR.

FLOREAT: Have they hit you? Oh you're bleeding.
(*She runs to cave mouth.*)
Stop! Stop shooting!

SON: Look, that must be its mate. A white bear. Shoot.
Shoot it for its valuable skin.
Shots.

FLOREAT: Stop shooting. It's me. Floreat.

FATHER: Stop shooting. Stop shooting.
(*He comes up.*)
It's you! Floreat! You're still alive!

FLOREAT: Of course I am! The bear fed me. He loves me
And I love him. Stop shooting, you've hurt him.

FATHER: What are you babbling about?

SON: The strain must have cracked her wits. She's loony.

FATHER: Pass me the heavy gun, I'll go in there
And finish off that monster.

FLOREAT: Stop, stop, stop!
The bear's fed me. Look at me.
I'm better. I'm happy. I'm cured.
Please stop and hear me.

FATHER: Floreat, what's going on?

SON: Who's that there in the cave, that young man?
Enter, from cave, youth carrying a bear's head and skin.

YOUTH: Will you let me explain?
There's a strange story to be told.

FLOREAT: Oh you're bleeding.

[70]

YOUTH: The bullet's broken my arm.
     I am the bear. I am the monster in the night.
     Give your belief time. For fifteen years
     I have been a bear in the sight of men and women.
     At all other times, a flying dragon.
     I would have been a bear and a flying dragon
     To the end of my days
     If Floreat had never said she loved me.
FLOREAT: Loved you!
YOUTH: Those were the words I needed to break the
     spell.
SON: But who was the bearkeeper?
YOUTH: He was illusion.
     I made you think you saw him. He was not there.
     This is the skin and the head of the bear that I was.
     This is the hole of the bullet you fired at the bear,
     Here in my arm.
FLOREAT: He's fainting. He's losing all that blood.
FATHER: Men, help him. Bring him along. We'll hear this
     story.
SON: He's a remarkably handsome fellow, for a bear.
FLOREAT: Take him gently, gently.
     Exeunt. Enter FLOORSWEEPER.
FLOORSWEEPER: Now there's going to be a wedding.
     Mightn't you have known.
     Well, I'll get roast chicken.
     And there'll be chicken for the cats,
     Which have all come running back with their tails
     in the air
     And for the dogs there'll be venison.
     Feeding, feeding, feeding,
     Sleeping, feeding and marrying –
     Trampling the floors, scattering the crumbs,

[71]

Somebody has to sweep them.
And the girl's recovered.
Why, it's simply amazing!
Her ailment's turned into a husband.
Wonders will never cease.

SEAN, THE FOOL, THE DEVIL
AND THE CATS

CHARACTERS

FOOL
MOTHER
SEAN
FIRST VOICE
SECOND VOICE
THIRD VOICE
FOURTH VOICE
CAT (miaowing)
DEVIL
MR POPPACOPOLIS
FIRST WORKER
SECOND WORKER
THIRD WORKER
MISS POPPACOPOLIS

SEAN, THE FOOL, THE DEVIL AND THE CATS

Music.

FOOL: Once upon a time – not very long ago – I was a happy
    man.
    But that's another story.
    Now I'm blind, I've no ears, I'm a quilt of scars.
    Look at me. Now listen.

    There was a boy called Sean.
    Not me. Sean was himself.
    I'm a fool. Sean was clever. Now listen.
    Sean was leaving home.

MOTHER: You're leaving me alone. O Sean, who'll look after
    me?

SEAN: The neighbours will look after you. Our savings will
    look after you. Goodbye, Mother.

MOTHER: O Sean, where will you go?
    Get a job in a bank, get a job on a farm,
    Get a job in a canning factory, keep out of harm.
    Get a job driving a lorry, if you want to see the
    world,
    But don't go away, don't leave me.

SEAN: I'm going for a year.

MOTHER: You're a dreamer, Sean. You stay at home. The
    world will eat you up.

SEAN: I'm going to try my luck. So wish me luck.

MOTHER: Don't go, Sean.

SEAN: I'm going.

MOTHER: Then may an angel go before you, an angel behind
    you,
    An angel to the right of you, an angel to the left,
    All lucky angels.

[75]

SEAN: Goodbye, Mother.

MOTHER: Write to me, write to me.

Music.

FOOL: Sean is on the road.

He walks at the roadside in the dust of the cars,
In the exhaust of the diesels,
The racket of the trucks. His head begins to ache.

SEAN: Where does the road go?

A road goes to a road.
Roads run into roads, fork into roads, circle and come
    back into roads.
Roads can never get away from roads.
Roads are a maze with no ending.
People who stick to the roads stick to the maze.
They all end up where they started.
Get off the road, Sean.

FOOL: Sean turns up a lane, over a hill,

Over a bridge, and he stops at a crossroads.
It is evening.

SEAN: The sun is setting. Where shall I sleep?

Four roads meet under my feet.
Which one shall I take?

FIRST VOICE (*very distant*): This way, Sean. This way for
happiness, Sean. We like you. We like you. This way for
smiles and presents and kisses.

SECOND VOICE (*distant*): This way, Sean, for thrills and
adventures. This way for hair on end and the skin of your
teeth and the luck of the devil. This way for the seven
deadly seas.

THIRD VOICE (*distant* – MOTHER's *voice*): Come home,
Sean, come home. Wait a year, go next summer, think
about it, remember your bed. Remember your old dog.
Remember my puddings.

FOURTH VOICE (*close and urgent*): This way, Sean, for a future. You're just the chap we need – the very man. Just what we're wanting – this way, Sean. There's a fortune in it. For you, Sean. A good sound job with a good sound future.

SEAN: Down every road of the four – there's a tempting voice. But what about that stile in the hedge? And the path that goes over the field beyond into that dark wood? That's a fifth way. How about that?

FIRST VOICE: No.

SECOND VOICE: No.

THIRD VOICE: Don't go that way, whatever you do.

FOURTH VOICE: Goodbye for ever, Sean, if you go that way.

SEAN: Why, what's wrong with it? It's only a path to a wood.

THIRD VOICE: No.

FOURTH VOICE: Don't go that way.

SEAN: Right, then I'll try it.

FOOL: Who's that? Halt. Give me a light.

SEAN: Did somebody speak? Or is it an escaped parrot?

FOOL: Down here in the ditch, fool. Under your feet. Can't you see what's under your feet?

SEAN: A face in the ditch. Can't you get out? Do you want a hand?

FOOL: Have you got a light?

SEAN: A match?

FOOL: A light – a lamp, a spot-light, something to see by – a torch. Haven't you got anything? Yes – a match, if you've got a match.

SEAN: I haven't got a match.

FOOL: Fool – wasting my time! How can I find my treasure if I haven't got a light? It's black as a mole-hole down here. I've got a pick, a mattock, a spade – I dig and I dig – but what's the use? I can't see a thing. I need a light.

SEAN: What is there to see?

FOOL: Treasure, fool, treasure. Here at the crossroads, a huge treasure. Have you never heard about it?

SEAN: No, I haven't.

FOOL: An enormous treasure somewhere here at the crossroads. Everybody knows about it. And everybody's too lazy to come and look for it. But I'm not too lazy. I'm no fool. I'm digging and I'm going to dig. But I need a light. Everybody who comes past here – I ask them for a light. Nobody ever has one. What is the matter with the world – everybody going round in the dark? Why doesn't anybody have a light? How can I see the treasure in the dark if I haven't got a light?

SEAN: You're the fool if you ask me. Are you going to dig the whole crossroads up?

FOOL: There's a huge treasure here somewhere. It's in all the old histories.

SEAN: Why, when you get it you'll be robbed, or you'll eat yourself to death. Or you'll be too old to enjoy it. Or you'll never get it at all. You'll just be an old worn-out ditch-digger – penniless.

FOOL: I can see you're jealous. Look: I've already found a shilling. I'm hot on the track. It's just that my luck's bad, that's all. In fact, my luck's rotten. What have you got in that bag?

SEAN: Sandwiches.

FOOL: I'll give you this shilling: you give me a sandwich.

SEAN: You give me your luck and the sandwich is yours. I don't want your shilling.

FOOL: You can have my luck. I give you my luck.

SEAN: And you can have a sandwich. Now I'm going over the stile.

FOOL: What – into the wood?

SEAN: Why not – if the path leads that way.

FOOL: Goodbye, Fool. You'll never come out alive – haven't you heard? There's a devilish Laughter in that wood.

SEAN: A what?

FOOL: A devilish screaming Laughter. Nobody goes near that wood. You hear it at night.

SEAN: Probably a woodpecker having a nightmare.

FOOL: It's the devil, fool. Don't mock him.

SEAN: I'm not scared of the devil. Or his cat. I'm off.

FOOL: Fool! Fool!

SEAN: Goodbye.

FOOL: Fool!

Music.

FOOL: Who was that fool in the ditch?

He went on digging for his treasure.

While Sean crossed the field in the twilight.

SEAN: I'm not scared of a dark wood. (*He whistles.*)

The wood gets darker. The wood is as dark as the fool's hole in the ditch. (*He whistles more softly.*)

FOOL: He enters the wood. He stops whistling.

He daren't whistle. The wood is too dark. And silent.

SEAN: The roots of the trees are like bridges, tunnels, caves. The tree-trunks twist away up, into dark. Here inside the wood, it's already dark. The path winds in, I can just see it. An owl floats up to stare. Little feet rustle in the fallen leaves. Ought I to go back? What's that?

(*A cat miaows.*)

A cat!

(*Cat miaows, closer.*)

Puss, puss, puss, are you lost? I see two huge eyes in the darkness. Are you a black cat? Do you live here? Cat, you

[79]

must be gigantic. Are you sure you're not a leopard –
with those eyes!
(*Cat miaows very close.*)
Is a black cat good luck or bad luck?
(*Miaow farther off.*)
The cat's going back, deeper into the wood.
(*Cat miaows, farther off, insistent.*)
Does it want me to follow? I'll follow it. A cat's a better
guide than none at all.
(*Cat miaows, farther off.*)
I'm coming, puss.

FOOL: Sean follows the cat.
He follows its miaows.
Sometimes he trips on a root, or snags his sleeve,
But he keeps going.
The cat comes to a clearing.
In the clearing – twilight again.
In the clearing – a house. Whose house?
Round, stone, a strange house.
The door is open. The cat goes in.
Sean follows the cat – into the strange house.
A strange one-roomed house.
A strange, vast fireplace, with a fire burning.
A strange, huge table – twice the size of a normal table.
A strange huge chair.
A strange huge bed.
A pan of stew, the size of a cauldron, bubbles on the
        fire.
The cat sits by the fire and it grins at Sean.
It's a cat the size of a big dog –
A strange huge cat.

SEAN: Who lives here, Cat?
Who's your master?

What a sumptuous smell, it makes me drool, the whiff of it.
Thieving or no thieving, I'll have some of that.
I'm hungry. And I'll eat.

FOOL: He eats. And he eats.
One bowlful isn't enough. Nor two. Nor three.

SEAN: What are you staring at, Cat?
Cat, your eyes are scary. They're too big.
Cat, you make me shiver.
Stop staring at me, Cat.
Here, have a bowl of stew.

FOOL: He gives the cat some stew. Look at that!!!!
He gives the cat some stew!!! He gives it some stew!!
Never forget that – give the cat some stew!

SEAN: Well, puss, we've cleared the lot up. What will your
master say to that? Who is your master? Why is
everything so big in this place? Look at this chair. Look at
that bed. Is he a giant? Look at those boots. Who could
wear such whiskery ugly boots – they look more like a
couple of muddy old sheepdogs, flopped out, dead-beat.
Does your master wear sheepdogs?

CAT: Miaow!

SEAN: What's that now, Cat? What is it?
(*Wild maniacal laugh in far distance – repeated coming
rapidly closer.*)
What – what – what's that? That's the Laughter. The
horrible Laughter. Is that your master, Cat? And is he
coming? I've eaten all the stew! I'd better hide. I can hear
the teeth in that laugh. Under the table. No. Inside one of
the boots? No. The chest, yes, into the chest. Don't tell
him, Cat, don't tell him where I've hidden.

FOOL: Sean jumps into the chest. It's full of old clothes.
He burrows under. He lowers the lid. He lies hidden.
Breathing like a little snake.

[81]

Maniacal laugh erupts into the room. It is the laughing
DEVIL, *as horrible as possible in all ways. He is panting*
and puffing among his laughs.

DEVIL: What a day! What a glorious day it's been! What a
wonderful day! Oh, I've had the time of my life. Any
visitors, Cat? There's a strange smell. Let me tell you: just
let me hear myself tell it all again. Listen. I've found a rich
man's beautiful daughter. Why are rich men's daughters
so beautiful? A strange fact, that is, very strange. And
this is a rich rich rich man's beautiful daughter. Miss
Poppacopolis!

And do you know what I've done? I've turned her into
a – CAT!

(*Wild shrieking laughs – subsides.*)

It's years since I had a day like this. The chances are
getting scarce, Cat. No good peppering people with the
plague, sweeping whole cities away with the smallpox,
levelling entire populations with paralysis – that's no
good. Not any more. Doctors come with their needles
and everybody's happy.

No. Now I strike for the mind. Not the body, the
mind. Now I make people crazy. I don't make them sick
any more, I make them crazy.

So now – instead of blasting this beautiful girl with
elephantiasis – I just throw a mouse in her face and
shout, 'You're a cat!' And now she thinks she's a cat.
She's gone cat-mad – she actually thinks that all she can
do is miaow and lap milk and run after mice.

(*Shrieks with uncontrollable laughter.*)

What's that smell? Has somebody been here, Cat?
Anyway, the girl will never be cured. Do you know
what the cure is? Who could ever guess it? Do you know
what it is? Three things. Three things.

Her father Mr Poppacopolis owns ten factories.
A whole town of factories. What sort of factories?
They can fruit. What sort of fruit?
Raspberries, strawberries, blackberries and plums.
Well, the profits are huge. How huge? Take my word
    for it
The profits of the factories are huge.
But the workers get only tiny wages.
Mr Poppacopolis keeps all the profits for himself. He's
    greedy.
That's why he keeps them: he's greedy.
And his workers get tiny wages.
So this is the first step in the cure:
Mr Poppacopolis has to share all his profits equally
    among all his workers.
So if the factories make more profit, they all make more
    money.
If they make less, they all make less.
Doesn't that sound sensible? Does it sound like one of the
    devil's ideas?
The point is: he'll never do it.
So his daughter will never be cured.

The second step is this:
All his workers line up in a long line,
Each holds a stick or an umbrella,
And Mr Poppacopolis
Has to run down the whole line of them,
And each one has to give him a whack.
There are thousands of workers – they'll kill him,
And he'll never do it. So his daughter will never be
    cured.

And the third and last step in the cure is this:

Somebody has to turn himself into a dog
And chase the rich man's daughter who thinks she's a cat
To the top of the fir tree in the middle of the rich man's
    garden.
At the top of that, hearing the barking
Of a dog that's no dog
The cat that's no cat
Will come to her senses and be cured.
But who'll ever think of doing that to cure her?
So she'll never be cured. Never. Never. O! O!
(*New shrieks of laughter – which suddenly stop.*)
Who's eaten my stew?
Cat, who's eaten my stew? Somebody's been here.
Somebody's eaten my stew. Stop grinning, Cat. Tell me.
Who? I'm going to die of rage. Who's eaten my stew?

FOOL: But he doesn't die. He rages and he rages. But after a
    while he falls on to the strange huge bed – and he snores.
    He snores, and as he snores he grinds his teeth.
    As soon as Sean hears him snoring, he lifts the lid of the
    chest.

SEAN: Goodbye, Cat.

FOOL: Out through the door. Away through the wood. Dark,
    black as the bottom of a swamp is the wood. He
    stumbles, he staggers, he drags himself up and he trips.

SEAN: Ouch!

FOOL: Thorns at his knees, knobbly snags at his temples.

SEAN: I'll have to get out of the wood before he wakes up.
    Ouch!

FOOL: He keeps going. He gropes. He feels his way.

SEAN: Now I need the fool's luck – no matter how bad. Ouch!

FOOL: All night he toils in the tangles of the undergrowth, the
    traps of the roots and the maze of the trunks. He is
    melting away with sweat. His heart bangs in his head.

[84]

He is ready to give up. When he sees –

SEAN: Dawn! A golden light in the grid of the trees. That must be the wood's edge and that must be dawn.

FOOL: He comes bursting out of the wood. And suddenly there are no trees, no roots, no tangle – only a wide smooth lawn. And he falls. He lies there gasping, in the dawn, in the dew. But somebody has seen him.

MR POPPACOPOLIS: Hoy there! Who's that? What are you up to? Hey!

FOOL: A big barrel of a man, like a kelly. With a bald head. A furious face, waddling in blue pyjamas that are covered with pink elephants. Walking in the dew before breakfast.

MR POPPACOPOLIS: This is a private garden. Trespassers prosecuted. Get out.

SEAN: I'm looking for Mr Poppacopolis.

MR POPPACOPOLIS: What do you want him for? At this hour of the morning.

SEAN: His daughter's ill.

MR POPPACOPOLIS: That's no news. She's ill all right. She's crazier every minute. Every doctor leaves her crazier than ever. She'll never be cured. The doctors have given her up. She's a lost cause. She thinks she's a cat! A beautiful girl – and she thinks she's a cat.

SEAN: I can cure her! You see how I'm torn to tatters? I've run all night – as the crow flies, a beeline straight through the forest. I couldn't lose a minute, because I've got the cure.

MR POPPACOPOLIS: What?

SEAN: I've got the cure.

MR POPPACOPOLIS: Cure? How can you cure her?

SEAN: Where's Mr Poppacopolis? Where is he?

MR POPPACOPOLIS: Come back. I'm him. Me. Walking here on my lawns because I'm going off my head with worry.

[85]

And you say you can cure her?

SEAN: Let me try. What can you lose? I dreamed it.

MR POPPACOPOLIS: You dreamed it?

SEAN: More or less. What can you lose? An angel told me in a
vision.

MR POPPACOPOLIS: An angel?

SEAN: And I remember it all.

MR POPPACOPOLIS: Quick. Get into action. If the angels are
on our side – there's hope. What do we do?

SEAN: First, you gather all your workers together . . .
Fading.

FOOL: But what's that noise? What's the uproar? Dawn,
6 a.m. and there's a horde of people coming up the
road. A cacophonous mob.
Roar of crowd – growing louder.

FIRST WORKER: Open the workshops.

SECOND WORKER: Open the doors.

THIRD WORKER: Let's get working. Let's get back to work.

ALL (*confusedly*): Open the workshops. Open the workshops.
Let's get back to work.

FIRST WORKER: Just because the boss's daughter's gone
crazy, he's closed down the factories. Can we stand for
that? He's closed down the factories so our wages have
stopped. Can we stand for that? Are the factories going
to stay closed till she gets better? Can we stand for that? I
say NO, NO and NO.

ALL: No, no, no. Open the workshops. Let's get back to work.

FIRST WORKER: His daughter might be mad for a lifetime.
Can we wait?

ALL: Open the factories, open the factories.

FIRST WORKER: We know he's worrying himself to death
over his daughter – but ought he to send all of us into
deep mourning, too?

[86]

ALL: No, no, no, she's not our daughter. Open the
   workshops.

FIRST WORKER: Mr Poppacopolis, come out. Get out of your
   bed and hear what we've got to say. If you don't open the
   factories we'll smash your house flat. What we can't
   smash, we'll burn. Then we'll smash the factories. Then
   we'll all migrate. If we can't work, we'll smash
   everything.
   (*Roar of crowd.*)
   Here he comes, here's the boss.

MR POPPACOPOLIS: Silence, everybody. Listen to me.
   Silence, everybody.

ALL: Shhhh! Hear what he's got to say. Let him have his
   say.

SECOND WORKER: It had better be good.

MR POPPACOPOLIS: Yes, I think it is good. Good news for
   you all. Listen patiently while I explain the new plan of
   operations . . . (*Fade.*)

FOOL: Where is Sean? Mr Poppacopolis is talking to the
   mob. He's waving his arms. He's counting off on his
   fingers. The terrible fierce mob is as quiet as a garden.
   Their faces are as astonished as the flowers. But where is
   Sean?

SEAN: Miss Poppacopolis, what a pretty cat you are!

MISS POPPACOPOLIS: Miaow!

SEAN: I've brought you your breakfast – a saucer of cream
   and a chicken leg. Your father sent me. He tells me you're
   called Katey.

MISS POPPACOPOLIS: Miaow!

SEAN: I saw a big dog in the hallway. Is he a friend or an
   enemy?

MISS POPPACOPOLIS: Miaow!

SEAN: Your father's talking to his workers. He's going to give

[87]

them a big present. He's going to stun them with a surprise. It's a big day for them. Oh, yes. All because of you. He's doing it for you, Katey.

MISS POPPACOPOLIS: Miaow!

Sudden thunderous hurrah, long and drawn out, merging into 'For he's a jolly good fellow', etc. Fading off as MR POPPACOPOLIS's *voice rises a little.*

MR POPPACOPOLIS: Silence, all! Quiet now! There's just one more thing. Don't let this surprise you . . . (*Fade.*)

SEAN: There, he's done it. Now he's going to let them all beat him – with sticks.

MISS POPPACOPOLIS (*distressed*): Miaow!

SEAN: Yes, he's going to let them all hit him as hard as they want – every one of them. In fact, he's asking them to.

MISS POPPACOPOLIS: Miaow!!!

SEAN: Don't worry! It's all in a good cause. It's a good job he gave them their present first – or they might have hit him a bit too hard. As it is – well, we'll see. Come on, eat your chicken, Katey.

MISS POPPACOPOLIS (*agitated*): Miaow! Miaow! Miaow!

SEAN: Don't worry about him. You see, it will all turn out –

MR POPPACOPOLIS (*entering*): I've done it. And I feel a million times better. And do you know, not one of them would hit me. I begged, I pleaded – finally they all just tapped me with a finger. Just a finger. It's all they'd do – tap me with a finger. That's loyalty for you, and affection. But will it be enough, do you think? Will it work?

SEAN: Have you shared out the factory profits?

MR POPPACOPOLIS: Just as you said.

SEAN: And every worker's tapped you with a finger?

MR POPPACOPOLIS: Is it enough?

SEAN: We'll see. Now for the third step, and the last.

SEAN and MISS POPPACOPOLIS, *sudden burst of barks, snarls, dog ravings – mingled with cat spittings, yowls, caterwauls, continuing.*

MR POPPACOPOLIS: Go easy with her – don't frighten her to death. Come back. Don't drive her into the woods, we might lose her for good. Come back! Katey! Katey!

FOOL: Sean is as much a dog as she is a cat. He snarls and foams at the mouth, she screeches and spits. She tears out of the room, bounds downstairs, jumps from the house, leaps across the garden, springs into the boughs of the fir tree. She climbs, she climbs, she climbs.

Sean snarls and barks and jumps at the bottom of the tree.

She climbs.

MR POPPACOPOLIS: Katey, don't fall! Be careful! Katey!

MISS POPPACOPOLIS: Daddy!

MR POPPACOPOLIS: What's that? Daddy? She said 'Daddy'. She spoke. She didn't miaow, she spoke.

MISS POPPACOPOLIS: O Daddy, get me down. How did I get up here? I'm in the top of this tree! I must have climbed up here in my sleep. Daddy, help. Daddy!

MR POPPACOPOLIS: She's cured! You've cured her! You miracle-worker! You magician! You absolute godsend! She's cured!

KATEY: Help! Help!

SEAN: Be still – I'm coming to get you.

FOOL: How does this story end? How do you think?

Sean ended up marrying that girl.

She couldn't get over him. He couldn't get over her.

Her father couldn't get over his relief.

The workers couldn't get over their luck.

Everybody was happy – except me. Me!

And what happened to me?

Sean came along the road with his wife, in his enormous
    car.

He was going to see his mother.

I was still digging in the ditch, at the crossroads.

Yes, that was me, still looking for my treasure.

He stopped, he called me up. He told me the whole story.

What would you have done?

Can't something like that happen to me? I thought, can't
    it all happen to me, too?

I threw down my pick, my mattock, my spade –

I ran over that field.

I ran into that wood.

I met that cat, just as Sean did. I followed the cat, just as
    Sean did.

I came to the strange round house, I went into the house.

I was hungry and there was the stew. I ate the stew, just as
    Sean did. I ate it. All of it. ALL of it!!!!

And I was licking the cauldron when that cat came across
    to me and gave me a great scratch.

I'd forgotten the cat!

I'd given no stew to the cat!!!

And straightaway the Laughter came, the horrible
Laughter. Just like Sean, I jumped into the chest.

The Laughter saw his stewpot empty. He asked the
miserable ugly cat who'd eaten it. The vile cross-eyed cat
betrayed me. The raging squash-headed disgusting beast
pointed to the chest I was in. And the Laughter dragged
me out. He dragged me out and he threw me to the cat –
that man-eater. And it clawed me. It hooked me and it
bit. I ran and the cat ran with me, raking and rending. I
ran and it ripped me to tatters. I got back to my
crossroads torn to tassels. I gave no stew to the cat, I'd

forgotten the cat, so it bit my ear off. I'd forgotten the cat, so it scratched my eyes out.
I'd forgotten the cat!
Never forget the cat!
If you want to prosper
Never forget the cat!
When you deal with the devil, never forget his cat!
Music.

ORPHEUS

CHARACTERS

NARRATOR
EURYDICE
ORPHEUS
FRIEND ONE
FRIEND TWO
FRIEND THREE
PLUTO
PERSEPHONE
VOICE
TREES
STONES

ORPHEUS

NARRATOR: This is the story
Of Orpheus the Magician, whose magic was music.
(*Music – guitar – pop.*)
This is the dance of the trees.
His music is so magic, he makes the trees dance.
The oaks unknot; they toss their limbs
And the willows whirl in a ring.
This is the dance of the trees.
(*Music stops. Giant sigh from all trees.*)
And this is the dance of the stones.
(*Music for stones – still pop.*)
His music is so magic the stones dance.
The rocks uproot and caper in their places,
The pebbles skip like mice,
The ordinary stones bounce like footballs.
This is the dance of the stones.
(*Music stops. Sigh from all stones.*)
His music reaches out to the bears in the forest.
(*Bear music – still pop.*)
It reaches up to the deer in the wrinkles of the hills.
(*Deer music.*)
It reaches down to the salmon in the pools below the
	falls.
(*Salmon music.*)
And wherever his music is heard, the dancing
	begins.
(*Music.*)
His music has a name. Its name is happiness.
Every living thing loves Orpheus
Because his music is happiness.
(*Eurydice becomes visible.*)

And this is the cause of Orpheus' happiness:
This is his wife, for her he makes his music.

ORPHEUS: Why shouldn't I be happy?
The world is beautiful.
Day after day the huge gift of the world
Is beautiful as ever.
More beautiful than the whole world is my wife
Eurydice.
This is the secret of my music.
It is all for Eurydice, my happiness.
Music.

NARRATOR: Nevertheless, there keeps coming a voice
To Orpheus – a voice which he does not like.

VOICE: Beware, Orpheus, beware.

NARRATOR: He dare not listen to the voice. He plays louder.
Music louder, to drown out the voice.

NARRATOR: Is it the voice of a bird? Or a spider? Or a
serpent?

VOICE (*very loud*): Beware, Orpheus, beware.
Music stops.

VOICE (*very soft*): Beware, beware, beware.

ORPHEUS: What should I beware of? Why should I beware?

VOICE: In the world of the trees,
In the world of the stones,
In the world of the frog, of the vole, of the linnet –
Every song has to be paid for.

ORPHEUS: Nonsense!
The world is a gift.
The brave take it with thanks and greet it with song.
Only the fearful peer at it with suspicion,
Thinking about the payment.

VOICE: Beware, Orpheus, beware.
Orpheus drowns the voice with a storm of his music.

NARRATOR: Orpheus hammers his guitar nevertheless.
And the trees dance once again
And the stones dance.
The deer on the hills, and the salmon in the weirs
And the bears in the holes of the forest
And the travellers out on the roads
Dance, dance when they hear it.
The world dances with happiness.
But suddenly –
Music falters and stops.

ORPHEUS: My hand! Something has happened to my hand.

NARRATOR: Orpheus' hand suddenly becomes numb.
*Sudden terrible cry in distance; voice coming nearer; a
friend bringing the news.*

FRIEND: Orpheus! (*Nearer.*) Orpheus!

ORPHEUS: Who is that?

FRIEND (*nearer*): Orpheus!

ORPHEUS: Here.

FRIEND (*very close, entering*): Orpheus!

ORPHEUS: Your face is terrifying. So is your voice.
What is your news?

FRIEND: Eurydice is dead.
*Magnified crash of strings, as if instruments smashed.
Light effects – sudden darkening.*

NARRATOR: Eurydice lies dead in the orchard, bitten by a
snake.
Her soul has left her body. Her body is cold.
Her voice has been carried away to the land of the
dead.

ORPHEUS: Eurydice!
*He lies prostrate. His music – now erratic and
discordant – struggles to tormented climax and again
collapses as if all instruments smashed. Light effects.*

[97]

NARRATOR: Orpheus mourns for a month and his music is
silent.

The trees droop their boughs; they weep leaves.

The stones in the wall weep.

The river runs silent with sorrow under its willows.

The birds sit mourning in silence on the ridge of the
house.

Orpheus lies silent and face downwards.

His friends try to rouse him.

FRIEND: Orpheus, you are mourning too long. The dead are
dead.

Remember the living. Let your own music heal your
sorrow.

Play for us.

NARRATOR: The trees know better.

TREES: We shall never dance again. Eurydice is dead.

Now we return to the ancient sadness of the forest.

NARRATOR: And the stones know better.

STONES: We are the stones, older than life. We have stood
by many graves. We know grief to the bottom. We danced
for a while because Orpheus was happy. Eurydice is
dead. Now we return to the ancient sadness of the
hills.

NARRATOR: But still his friends try to rouse him.

FRIENDS ONE, TWO and THREE: Eurydice did not want you
to grieve so long, Orpheus. Play your music again.
Deceive your grief. Defeat evil fortunes. The dead
belong to the dead, the living to the living. Play for
us.

NARRATOR: Have they succeeded?

At last! Orpheus reaches for the magic strings.

*One note, repeated, gathering volume and impetus –
insane.*

FRIENDS ONE, TWO and THREE: Horrible! Is this music?
　He has forgotten how to play. Grief has damaged his
　brain. This is not music.
ORPHEUS: I am going down to the underworld.
　To find Eurydice.
FRIENDS: Mad! He is mad! Orpheus has gone mad!
ORPHEUS: I am going to the bottom of the underworld.
　I am going to bring Eurydice back.
FRIEND ONE: Nobody ever came back from the land of the
　dead.
ORPHEUS: I am going. And I shall come back.
　With Eurydice.
FRIENDS: Mad! He is mad! Orpheus has gone mad!
　Nobody ever returns from the land of the dead.
　Their voices fade. His crazy note strengthens,
　modulating into electronic infernal accompaniments.
　Major light effects through what follows.
NARRATOR (*speaking with greatly magnified voice over*
　the music – not declaiming so much as a giant
　whisper):
　Where is the land of the dead? Is it everywhere? Or
　　nowhere.
　How deep is the grave?
　What is the geography of death?
　What are its frontiers?
　Perhaps it is a spider's web. Perhaps it is a single grain
　　of dirt.
　A million million souls can sit in an atom.
　Is that the land of the dead?
　A billion billion ghosts in the prison of an atom
　Waiting for eternity to pass.
　(*Orpheus music louder. Light effects.*)
　Orpheus beats his guitar. He is no longer making music.

He is making a road of sound. He is making a road
through the sky. A road to Eurydice.

ORPHEUS: Eurydice! Eurydice! Eurydice!

NARRATOR: He flies on his guitar. His guitar is carrying him.
It has lifted him off the earth. It lifts him over the
treetops.

*Music continuing, the monotonous note like a drum note
insistent.*

FRIENDS: Orpheus, come back! Orpheus, come back!

ORPHEUS: Eurydice!

NARRATOR: It carries him into a cloud.

(*Light and sound effects through what follows, his music
continuing throughout.*)

Through the thunder he flies. Through the lightning.
It carries him
Through the storm of cries,
The last cries of all who have died on earth,
The jealous, screaming laments
Of all who have died on earth and cannot come back.
Storm of cries.

ORPHEUS: Eurydice!

NARRATOR: He lays his road of sound across the heavens.
His guitar carries him.
Into the storm of blood,
The electrical storm of all the blood of all who have died
on earth.
He is whirled into the summit of the storm.
Lightnings strike through him, he falls –

ORPHEUS: Eurydice!

NARRATOR: He falls into the mouth of the earth.
He falls through the throat of the earth, he recovers.
He rides his serpent of sound through the belly of the
earth.

He drives his spear of sound through the bowels of the
  earth.
Mountains under the earth fall on him, he dodges.
He flies through walls of burning rock and ashes.
His guitar carries him.
(*Music continuing monotonous and insane.*)
He hurtles towards the centremost atom of the earth.
He aims his beam of sound at the last atom.
ORPHEUS: Eurydice!
NARRATOR: He smashes through the wall of the last atom.
  He falls
  He falls
  At the feet of Pluto, king of the kingdom of the dead.
  Silence. Appropriate light effects.
PLUTO: So you have arrived. At first I thought it was a fly.
  Then I thought it was a meteorite. But now I see – it is a
  man. A living man, in the land of the dead. Stand. I am
  Pluto, king of the underworld. And you, I think, are
  Orpheus.
NARRATOR: Orpheus stands on the floor of the hall of
  judgement, like a mouse on the floor of a cathedral.
  Pluto's face, vast on his vast throne, is made of black
  iron, and it is the face of a spider. The face of Persephone,
  his wife and queen, vast on her vast throne, beside him, is
  made of white ivory, and it is the pointed, eyeless face of
  a maggot.
PLUTO: Orpheus! I have heard of you. What is it, Orpheus,
  brings you alive to the land of the dead?
ORPHEUS: You took away my wife Eurydice.
PLUTO: That is true.
ORPHEUS: What can I do to get her back?
PLUTO: Get her back? (*Laughs – Plutonic laughter in
  hell.*)

[101]

Alas, your wife has gone into the vaults of the dead.
You cannot have her back.

ORPHEUS: Release her. You are a god. You can do as you like.

PLUTO: Some things are not in my power, Orpheus. Here is
my wife, for instance, Persephone. Perhaps you have
heard about her. Six months she spends with me, here in
the underworld. Six months she is up on earth, in the
woods and meadows, with her mother. That is the
arrangement. Up on the earth she is a flower-face, she
laughs and sings; everybody adores her. But now you see
her. Here in the underworld she is quite different. She
never makes a sound. Never speaks, never sings. And you
see her face? It is the peaked face of a maggot. Yet it is not
a maggot. It is the white beak of the first sprout of a
flower. I have never seen it open. Here in the underworld
it is closed – white, pointed and closed – the face of a
maggot.

Here is something I cannot alter.

There is another thing, Orpheus. Here in the underworld,
the accounting is strict. A payment was due from you.

ORPHEUS: Payment?

PLUTO: Nothing is free. Everything has to be paid for. For
every profit in one thing – payment in some other
thing. For every life – a death. Even your music – of
which we have heard so much – that had to be paid for.
Your wife was the payment for your music. Hell is now
satisfied.

ORPHEUS: You took my wife –

PLUTO: To pay for your music.

ORPHEUS: But I had my music from birth. I was born with it.

PLUTO: You had it on credit. You were living in debt. Now
you have paid, and the music is yours.

ORPHEUS: Then take back my music. Give me my wife.

PLUTO: Too late.

ORPHEUS: What good is my music without my wife?
What can I do to make you give me my wife?

PLUTO: Nothing can open Hell.
(*Orpheus strikes a chord – no longer pop –
solemn Handel, Bach, Vivaldi or earlier. Light
effects.*)
Now what are you doing?
Your music is even more marvellous in Hell.
Than ever on earth. But it cannot help you.
Music.

ORPHEUS: Look at your wife, Pluto. Look at Persephone,
your queen.
Music.

PLUTO: Her face is opening.

ORPHEUS: A wife for a wife, Pluto. Shall I continue to
play?

PLUTO: Keep playing. Keep playing.
(*Music stops.*)
Keep playing. Why have you stopped?

ORPHEUS: It is in my power to release the flower
in your wife's face and awake her. Release my wife.

PLUTO: Play.

ORPHEUS: A wife for a wife.

PLUTO: Whatever you wish. Only play. You can have your
wife.
Music.

PLUTO: Beautiful as the day I plucked her off the earth!
Music stops.

ORPHEUS: You have your wife, Pluto.

PERSEPHONE: Keep your promise, to Orpheus. Give him
his wife.

PLUTO: I cannot.

ORPHEUS: Cannot? A god cannot break his promise.
   A god's promise is stronger than the god.
PLUTO: I cannot. Your wife's body is crumbling to dust.
PERSPEPHONE: Give him her soul.
PLUTO: I can only give you her soul.
ORPHEUS: Let it be so. Let my wife's soul come with me.
   Light effects. Dance and mime through what follows.
PLUTO: You who have awakened the queen of Hell,
   Return to the world. Your wife's soul will be with you.
   Orpheus' new music very soft.
NARRATOR: Orpheus returns to the earth. It is not far. It is
   only a step.
   A step, a step, and a step,
   A step – and he turns. He looks for his wife. The air
   is empty.
   Music stops.
ORPHEUS: Eurydice?
EURYDICE: I am here.
ORPHEUS: Eurydice, where are you? Eurydice?
EURYDICE: Here at your side, Orpheus.
NARRATOR: He cannot see her. He cannot touch her. He can
   only hear her. He listens.
EURYDICE: Play for me, Orpheus.
   Orpheus plays his new music.
NARRATOR: Orpheus' friends come running. They listen to
   his music. It is no longer the same music.
FRIEND ONE: This won't make anybody dance.
FRIEND TWO: This is queer music. He's gone to the dogs.
   This is dreary.
FRIEND THREE: Play as you used to play, Orpheus. Make us
   dance.
   Music continues.
NARRATOR: The trees did not dance. But the trees listened.

The music was not the music of dancing
But of growing and withering,
Of the root in the earth and the leaf in the light,
The music of birth and of death.
And the stones did not dance. But the stones listened.
The music was not the music of happiness
But of everlasting, and the wearing away of the hills,
The music of the stillness of stones,
Of stones under frost, and stones under rain, and stones
     in the sun,
The music of the seabed drinking at the stones of the
     hills.
The music of the floating weight of the earth.
And the bears in their forest holes
Heard the music of bears in their forest holes,
The music of bones in the starlight,
The music of many a valley trodden by bears,
The music of bears listening on the earth for bears.
And the deer on the high hills heard the crying of wolves,
And the salmon in the deep pools heard the whisper of
     the snows,
And the traveller on the road
Heard the music of love coming and love going
And love lost forever,
The music of birth and of death.
The music of the earth, swaddled in heaven, kissed by its
     cloud and watched by its ray.
And the ears that heard it were also of leaf and of stone.
The faces that listened were flesh of cliff and of river.
The hands that played it were fingers of snakes and a
     tangle of flowers.

THE PIG ORGAN

CHARACTERS

THE KING
THE PRINCESS
BELICANTA
OTTO
THE FRIAR
SCHWEINSHREKKER
COURT MUSICIAN
MARIGOLD, the dancing piglet
THE PIGLETS – Orange-blossom, Honeysuckle,
Snowdrop, Rose-petal, Meadowsweet

PUBLISHER'S NOTE

The original text contains indications for operatic production. Each of the characters is given a voice: The King: Baritone, The Princess: Soprano, Belicanta: Mezzo-soprano, Otto: Tenor, The Friar: Bass, Schweinshrekker and The Court Musician: Tenor. Instruments, which were intended to surround and participate in the action 'in the manner of a small court orchestra', are grouped in pairs: Flute (also piccolo and alto flute) and Clarinet (also Bass Clarinet); Trumpet and Trombone (also 'Belliphon'); Percussion and Harp; Violin (also 'Swionin') and Cello.

We have placed the musical terms, which occur throughout – *duet, aria, musical interlude*, etc. – in square brackets. The lines can just as well be said as sung, but we felt that the musical instructions might help with the tone, or indicate the sort of stage business going on. The play can be imagined perhaps like a modern-day masque, where acting and music are mixed together in the telling of the story.

THE PIG ORGAN

[*Prelude: The Dance of the Little Pig*]

SCENE I

The new instrument, fantastically constructed, is wheeled in, incredibly top-heavy and teetering. Adjustments are made through what follows.
[*Duet:*]

COURT MUSICIAN: At last – it is finished! Finished! Finished!

At last it is finished!

Finished for the King!

BELICANTA: Keep calm, my dear, keep calm.

The doctor said keep calm –

COURT MUSICIAN: The King's Birthday Present!

My glorious invention!

BELICANTA: Keep calm, my dear, keep calm!

COURT MUSICIAN: For the King!

This glorious machine.

Machinery that sings.

Music has found the wings

To fly into the new age and the starry spaces!

VOICE: The King!

BELICANTA: His Majesty. Now keep calm.

VOICE: The King!

Enter MARIGOLD, *the little pig, dancing around the instrument.*

BELICANTA: What is it?

COURT MUSICIAN: Is it human?

BELICANTA: It's a kobbold!

COURT MUSICIAN: It's a goblin!

BELICANTA: Looks like a pig. Surely it's a pig.

COURT MUSICIAN: It must be bewitched. A witch's
    pig.

VOICE: His Majesty the King!

COURT MUSICIAN: Out! Animal! Out!

BELICANTA: The King is coming –

COURT MUSICIAN: Out! Out! Out!
    The creature's accursed.

BELICANTA: The creature's possessed.

COURT MUSICIAN: Demonic!

BELICANTA: Malignant!
    What does this mean?
    This is an omen! An omen! An omen!

COURT MUSICIAN: It's wrecking my machine.

BELICANTA: O Heaven help us!

COURT MUSICIAN: Where is my axe?
    I'll split his minims!
    I'll chip him, I'll chop him,
    I'll mince him to demi-semi-quavers!

BELICANTA: Don't apoplex!

VOICE: Her Highness, the Princess.

    COURT MUSICIAN *chases* MARIGOLD, *his axe
    raised. Enter* PRINCESS. MARIGOLD *rushes to*
    PRINCESS, *who conceals it under her billowing
    gown.* COURT MUSICIAN, *axe aloft, confronts*
    PRINCESS.

PRINCESS: Stop! Don't harm that pig!

VOICE: His Majesty, the King!
    Enter KING.

KING: Musician! Conduct yourself!

BELICANTA: Your Majesty, forgive him!
    That pig is to blame –
    Was wrecking Your Majesty's present.

This magnificent
Birthday-beautiful
Miracle-harmony
Music-machine.
That pig is bewitched. It was driving us wild.
KING: Adagio, maestro!
Ignore the little devil.
Now – what is this thing?
COURT MUSICIAN: A machine, a marvel
That listens
To the music
Of the atoms in their spheres,
And softens it
And mixes it
And warms it
And shapes it
To the shape of human ears.
KING: Let me hear it! Let me hear
The music of the atoms.
What a wonderful present!
COURT MUSICIAN *tunes and plays the instrument.*
[*Aria bel canto*:]
BELICANTA: The Lark has hung her harpsichord
A dangle from the burning Sun.
The Nightingale plucks at the Moon
Until the ghostly night is done.

Our earth itself it is a lute
On which the bending heavens finger,
(MARIGOLD *emerges and begins to dance, at first to the
music of the aria, then seeming to conjure her own music
out of the instrument, in spite of the* COURT
MUSICIAN'*s efforts to hold his own.* BELICANTA *sings*

[111]

*more and more strongly against the pig music, finally
ending in a scream.*)
Our earth itself it is a lute
    On which the bending heavens finger,
Human music is the voice
    Of Almighty God the Singer.
(COURT MUSICIAN *has raised his axe again, raises it
over his head, rushes at the pig – falls dead. With a
tremendous crash all sounds cease.* MARIGOLD
vanishes.)
My husband! Oh, my husband's dead!
That pig was a devil! It has killed my husband!
KING: Guards. Catch that pig. Find the pig's owner. Bring
    back both. Execute both.
[*Trio doloroso:*]
My old Musician dead? Oh!
Where shall I find music?
PRINCESS: The old Musician dead?
How will my father live without music?
The old Musician dead?
He cannot be dead, he cannot be dead.
BELICANTA: My husband dead – Oh!
He shall be buried under a willow
Where the leaves shall mourn all summer.
And all winter the boughs shall weep
Into a sleepless river of sorrow:
A silent river and a harp of sighs.
KING: Left foot, right foot,
The slow nightmare
With a sackful of disaster
Climbs up the stair.
The left foot's fallen.
One man is dead.

[112]

The right foot's lifted
O where will it tread?

BELICANTA: My husband dead – Oh!
And on Your Majesty's birthday.
This was my husband's happiest day,
The organ was his masterpiece.

PRINCESS: Music must be found.
Without music father will not eat.
Without music, like a fire
Without fuel, he will perish.
Music must be found.
Without music he cannot sleep.
Without music, like a flower
Without water, he will wither.
Music must be found.

MARIGOLD *re-emerges and runs over the body of
the* COURT MUSICIAN.

KING: That accursed pig. Find it! Catch it!

Exit PRINCESS *after* MARIGOLD, *exit rest
separately.*

[*Musical Transition.*]

SCENE 2

The swineherd OTTO, *at a distance, sings,
approaching.*
[*Aria ritornello:*]

OTTO: O pretty is the little pig
    As pretty as a flower
As pink as the pink rose
    In the rose-bower
And sweet as the honeysuckle
    Hanging on the wall

Of all God's flowers the little pig
      Is prettiest of all.
[*Ritornello*] (*during which he calls for his* PIGLETS.
Enter MARIGOLD *followed by* PRINCESS. MARIGOLD
runs to OTTO *who embraces it.* PRINCESS *remains
concealed*).
God is angry – and it's thunder
      Sad – and the sea sighs
But it is the little pig
      When God cries
The lightning is too swift
      And the sea too wild
On a little pig's feet
      God walks the world.
[*Ritornello*] (PRINCESS *approaches* OTTO, *now
surrounded by his* PIGLETS. OTTO, *captivated by the*
PRINCESS *sings the last verse to her*).
OTTO: Silent is the grave
      Silent is the star.
It's the little pig's song
      Tells you where you are.
O raindrops in the cloud
      And water in the sea
And love in the little pig
      Is all there can be.
PRINCESS: You must escape. You have no time to lose.
OTTO: Who are you?
PRINCESS: The King has ordered your execution. His
      guards are hunting for you and your pig. You must
      hide.
OTTO: Execution? I have not committed any crime. How can
      an innocent pig be guilty?
PRINCESS: Your pig killed a man.

OTTO: Killed a man? Marigold? Killed a man? My little pig?
Noise offstage. Exit PIGLETS *squealing.* MARIGOLD *remains.*

PRINCESS: Can't you hear? The King has ordered your execution.

OTTO: I demand to speak to the King.

PRINCESS: You have to believe me – the King is my father.

OTTO: You – are – the Princess?
Noise offstage.

PRINCESS: Here, hide your pig here.
She hides MARIGOLD *under her billowing gown. Enter* SCHWEINSHREKKER.

SCHWEINSHREKKER: Have you seen a pig? A mad pig? A
witchy pig?
Probably with red sparkling eyes?
Probably with a fork in its tail?
Here are the ugly hoofprints
Of a beast of the wanted type.
The pig is in the vicinity.
Princess, have you seen the pig?

PRINCESS: That way! Hurry! They ran! Together!

SCHWEINSHREKKER: That pig's head is as good as off and
dangling from the butcher's hook. And its owner's head
is rocking. (*to* OTTO) Who are you?

OTTO: I once saw a pig in a bath.

SCHWEINSHREKKER: Oaf!
Exit SCHWEINSHREKKER.

PRINCESS: You heard what he said,
Now run, run, run.

OTTO: You the Princess! Why should you save me?

PRINCESS: They are coming back. Wake up! Wake up!

OTTO: Several thunderbolts are flying in the air
And all of them are trying to hit me –

Enter SCHWEINSHREKKER.

PRINCESS: You've missed them again. That way!

    Exit SCHWEINSHREKKER.

    [*Duet:*]

PRINCESS: A thunderbolt eagle

    Has swooped and picked me up off the earth.

    It carries me high into a dazzling –

    O am I falling?

    The candle's flame, the bonfire's smoke

    Go upward, go blindly,

    And souls from bodies – O am I falling?

    I have lost myself in love with a swineherd!

OTTO: A chain like a mountain has fallen on me

    My freedom's gone, I cannot escape,

    The eyes of a Princess have locked me up.

    Some fall into the fire

    Some fall into the sea

    Some fall off the world and fall

    Everlastingly.

    But I have fallen in love with a Princess.

    Enter SCHWEINSHREKKER.

SCHWEINSHREKKER: Princess, P-P-P-Princess!

PRINCESS: Now what's the matter?

SCHWEINSHREKKER: Your father!

PRINCESS: What? Don't frighten me!

SCHWEINSHREKKER: Something t-t-t . . .

PRINCESS: What is it, what is it?

SCHWEINSHREKKER: . . . terrible!

PRINCESS: Father? O what's happened?

    Exit PRINCESS *and* SCHWEINSHREKKER.

OTTO: I shall hide here

    Inside old age

    So while the King rages

I'll know she is near.

OTTO *puts on a beard, cloak and wide-brimmed hat as he sings, eventually resembling an old, crippled man.*

[*Musical Transition.*]

SCENE 3

KING (*offstage, roaring with rage*): Doctors! Medicine!
   Useless, useless! Nothing can cure me!
   Enter SCHWEINSHREKKER.
SCHWEINSHREKKER: The King is sick
   With a strange sickness!
   I have to look in every book!
   The King has a sickness
   Which does not exist!
   Enter KING.
KING: Every hour my sickness grows worse.
   I watch the clock like the wheel of a hearse.
   Nobody knows what my ailment is.
   Find its name! Name it! Name it!
   Let me know how sick I am.
   Enter PRINCESS.
PRINCESS: Father, listen, it's music you're missing.
   Music heals everything.
   And you know that you need music.
KING: My music is dead. Killed by a pig!
PRINCESS: My father is changing – hourly, horribly.
   Aria:
KING: My old Musician made the most
         Fantastic instruments
   And when he played he soothed the souls
         Of maddened elephants

[117]

And parrots stopped their swearing and
    Monkeys pulled up their pants.

But this silence is a drum
    That summons dreadful things:
Wolf-hair sprouts on maidens' cheeks
    And a gorilla swings
From the family tree and boars' ears
    Push the crowns off kings.

    Look at my hand. It's no longer a hand.
    That hand is a hoof. Do you see? A hoof?
    What is the sickness where hands become hooves?
SCHWEINSHREKKER: Perhaps it's a callus.
KING: A callus?
SCHWEINSHREKKER: Yes.
KING: A callus? It's a hoof.
    It's plainly the hoof of a pig.
SCHWEINSHREKKER: It's a callus.
    A peculiar callosity and quite common.
KING: Now I know. I shall be a carcase
    Of common
    Peculiar
    Complete
    Callus.
    Nothing will cure me! I'll be one great hoof!
    [*Trio:*]
SCHWEINSHREKKER: The King is sick
    With a strange sickness.
    The King has a sickness
    That does not exist.
KING: Every hour my sickness grows worse.
    I watch the clock like the wheel of a hearse.
    Nobody knows what my ailment is.

Find its name. Name it! Name it!
Let me know how sick I am.
PRINCESS: My father is changing –
Hourly, horribly.
Enter BELICANTA.
BELICANTA: I bring you the cure!
Your Majesty, your servant
Brings you the cure!
This my duty to my dead husband.
I told the Friar
You are possessed by a devil
In the shape of a pig!
Enter FRIAR.
FRIAR: Silence! The power of the Lord
Descends upon the land
And is at hand.
Tremble demons in your jelly mould!
You in the King's belly! You are rumbled!
Cymbals!
(BELICANTA *clashes cymbals.*)
Name thyself, devil! Name thyself!
BELICANTA: Name yourself, devil, name yourself!
FRIAR: Name thyself!
[*Quintetto:*]
BELICANTA: Say something, devil!
FRIAR: I exorcise thee, hog-trotter, streaky, tripe-guts,
swine-chops,
In the name of the Lamb!
BELICANTA: Hit him with it! Knock it out of him!
FRIAR: Vomit thyself, regurgitate,
Eructate and spew out
Thy chines, thy fries, thy puddings, black and white,
Thy back and belly pork, thy chitterlings.

[119]

FRIAR *struggles with the* KING, *forcing him to eat a roast of lamb.*

BELICANTA: He's a stubborn devil! Give it to him!

FRIAR: Out, thy glutton of brine, thou monster of oak-smoke,

Out, thy devil of salted sage and onion,

Who scaleth the Lord's annointed with burnt crackling.

Trampler of sanctity!

Quadruple cleft of cacophony!

Split-hoof! Out!

BELICANTA: Beat him! Drive him out! Beat him!

SCHWEINSHREKKER: That's enough! Stop! Stop!

PRINCESS: Stop him! Stop him! Father!

FRIAR: We're nearly there!

BELICANTA: Strangle him!

FRIAR: I feel his strength!

KING: Help!

SCHWEINSHREKKER *wrestles with the* FRIAR. KING *hits* FRIAR *and frees himself.* KING *holds up his other hand, which is now also a hoof.*

KING: Aaaah!

Exit KING, *waving his hooves and screaming.*

PRINCESS (*to* FRIAR): You're the curse. You've made him worse.

You're the devil. Out! Out!

Exit.

SCHWEINSHREKKER: The King's sickness is out of control.

This is horrible!

Exit.

SCENE 4

FRIAR *and* BELICANTA *are left in a heap on the floor.*

FRIAR: Ecce ecce Agnus Dei
   Huc eat et illuc
   Valva deicto obice
   Rumpatque postes
   Perlucet omnis regia
   His vides abditum
   Natum scelesti patri.

BELICANTA: O what can be done?

FRIAR: Ecce ecce Corpus Agni
   Licet tonantis profuga
   Condaris sinu
   Petet undecumque
   Temet haec dextra et feret
   Eloquere nomen.
   Diabolo. Eloquere nomen.

BELICANTA: Ah! I have it!
   We must have a competition
   For a new Court Musician.

FRIAR: A competition for a new Court Musician?
   [*Duet:*]

BELICANTA: All through the land
   We will have a competition
   For a new Court Musician.

FRIAR: I see it in a vision
   This job – is – for me.
   I shall win the competition
   For a new Court Musician.
   The King will appoint me
   The Princess will applaud me
   Belicanta will adore me.

BELICANTA: Adore you?
  When you come near me I feel the ground tremble.
  And when you speak I feel I'll be squashed.
  And when you look at me I quake to custard.
  I feel you want to eat me!
  With guzzling sucks of your great red lips!
  Or else tip me up, and then gulp me down
  Into your shaking and booming belly
  As if I were a trifle.
  It makes me giddy to think of him.
FRIAR: Blasphemous – but beautiful!
  Come to my feast, lady, come to my feast!
  Your coiffure will be a crown of lamb
  Your bosoms a beautiful baron of beef
  Around your neck a great necklace of oysters.
  Come to my feast, lady, come to my feast.

  With a benison of venison we'll cast away care,
  We'll stuff our soles with sirloin of salmon
  And rejoice in the Lamb with roast goose and gammon
  Till the goodness drips down from our elbows and hair.
  A mousse of bass, a mess of eels
BELICANTA: A bouillabaisse of halibut
FRIAR: Turbot a pretty pot or two
BELICANTA: And walloping dollops of scallops and mussels.
FRIAR: A six-foot lobster on a spit
BELICANTA: And caviare to cover us
FRIAR: Duck and woodcock packed with oysters
BELICANTA: And sweetbreads and prawns, and brains and
    sea urchins.
  And truffle-stuffed pheasants and snails by the pailful
FRIAR: And sirloin in ale and burgundy hare
BOTH: And suckling piglet all basted in honey.

Enter MARIGOLD, *dancing.*

BELICANTA: The pig! It's the pig!

FRIAR: It's that dancing diabolical pig again!

Exit FRIAR *and* BELICANTA *chasing* MARIGOLD.

[*Musical Transition.*]

SCENE 5

Enter OTTO, *searching for* MARIGOLD, *still wearing his disguise.*

OTTO: Marigold! Marigold!

O who came in without a care,
    But a jolly fat pig with its bum all bare
With flip-flop ears, and pretty little toes
    With an eye like an elf and a roly-poly nose.

Enter PRINCESS.

PRINCESS: I thought I heard –
    I'm certain I heard –
    Are you alone?

OTTO: I've lost a piglet.

PRINCESS: O what's happened to Otto?
    Do you know Otto?
    I just heard his song.
    I'll swear I heard it.

OTTO: We all sing the song the pigs know best.

PRINCESS: Where is he?

OTTO: Vanished.

PRINCESS: Where to?

OTTO: Far, far, far, where the sows grow wool
    And every nisseldraft's big as a bull.

PRINCESS: Tell me. Can a letter reach him?

OTTO: What is your message? I'll see he gets it.

[123]

PRINCESS: I must see him. Speak to him. Hear him.
    [*Duet:*]
OTTO: See him?
PRINCESS: See him.
OTTO: Speak to him?
PRINCESS: Yes, speak to him.
OTTO: Hear him?
PRINCESS: O yes, hear him!
OTTO: And he must come to you?
PRINCESS: He must, O yes he must!
OTTO: Because you love him?
PRINCESS: Yes, I love him.
        OTTO *takes off his disguise.*
PRINCESS: O what have I said?
OTTO: Your message arrived
        Your message flew
        A million miles
        An impossible journey
        At miracle speed
        And worked a miracle.
PRINCESS: Once I was a princess
        Now I am a leaf
        A blade of grass
        The most humble soul
        Blown this way and that
        By breathings of love.
        Once I was queenly
        And lofty and witty
        Love's stripped me bare
        As a reed in the river.
OTTO: What was heavy as lead and ruined as
            wrong
        Is brighter than gold and right as a song

Your message has made an old man young.

I talked to the trees
I prayed to the birds
I asked my pigs
To plead with the earth.
My hopelessness
The darkest, coldest
Hour before dawn.
The sun heard me.
My love moved the sun.
The sun has answered me
Through your mouth.
PRINCESS: I heard nothing
I saw nothing
I said nothing
I did nothing
I was blinded
Deafened, dumb.
I was helpless.
As if I had stepped
Into the sun
I met love.
Nothing is left of me but
Brighter, brighter love.
OTTO: The river of my love
Shall wash us for ever.
*A dreadful wailing is heard offstage – crashes and
breaking glass.*
PRINCESS: My father – O my father.
Speak to him,
Tell him everything.
Another dreadful cry offstage.

OTTO: . . . I cannot
    . . . I dare not
    Exit OTTO *and* PRINCESS *separately as* KING
    approaches.

[*Musical Transition.*]

SCENE 6

Enter KING.
KING: There is no hope.
    There is no hope.
    There is no hope.
    Hour by hour, limb by limb, I am being changed.
    Strange rippling sensations
    Crawl through my body,
    And the strangest speculations
    Float into my head.

    How many boiled potatoes in a pood?
    How many chomps
    In a snuffle of truffles?
    Which is the slurpiest –
    Mash or mush?

    Which is the most majestic mattress,
    Plain mud or midden?

    My hand and my hand
    My ear and my ear
    And my two feet –

    Strange phrases itch in my ears like fleas:
    A rat in claret?
    Tomcat tartare?

Dead dog jugged?
Enter PIGLETS *carrying poles with grotesque pigs'*
heads, and monstrous pork pies with which they
bombard the KING.

KING: I dream I am damned:
One great devil
Is a bacon-slicer.
Many small devils
Are kebab skewers.
I saw Satan
A sausage machine.
I saw Hell:
It has a crust
Like a burnt pork pie.

What is happening to me?
Schweinshrekker.
Where are you?
Where are you?
Schweinshrekker.
PIGLETS *vanish. Enter* SCHWEINSHREKKER.

SCHWEINSHREKKER: It cannot be denied
The King is becoming a –
His hooves, his cleft hooves
His cleft and tiptoe hooves
Are the hooves of a –
It has to be declared
It cannot be denied.
His ears, O his ears
His hairy flip-flop ears
Are the ears of a –
It cannot be denied
The King is becoming a –

KING: Maybe I'm becoming a phoenix.
    A unicorn, a pelican,
    A rare caladrius,
    A dirty, shaggy sheep!

    A common creaking crocodile
    Crusted all in crinkled callous
    Crawling like a caterpillar tank
    To marry a gharial!

SCHWEINSHREKKER: Medicine's amazed,
    Prescription's bankrupt,
    The herbal's hopeless,
    So what remains?

KING: Shall I be a horse?
    A bull or billy-goat?
    Shall I be a camel?
    A stag or buffalo?
    (*A march is heard in the distance.*)
    What's that?
    What noise is that?

    [*March.*]

SCENE 7

Enter BELICANTA *and* PRINCESS. *The band approaches.*

BELICANTA: With Your Majesty's permission
    The competition will begin
    For a new Court Musician.

KING: I don't like their faces
    And I shan't like their noise.

PRINCESS: Please be patient, father.

BELICANTA: Musicians are notorious

For their ugly faces.
A genius is a monster.
They have to pay something
For their unearthly souls.

KING: I am ready to be tortured.

SCHWEINSHREKKER: These are the candidates? Hopeless!

BELICANTA: You will all perform in turn
And the King shall be your judge.
Get your instruments ready.
Perform in turn . . . You begin.
FIRST MUSICIAN performs 'The Belliphon Sonata'.
The KING is impassive. MUSICIAN tries again.

PRINCESS: Enough.

SCHWEINSHREKKER: Hopeless!

BELICANTA: Next.

PRINCESS: And please do your best.
*SECOND MUSICIAN performs 'The Swionin
Sonata'.*

KING: Stop!
Am I getting better?

PRINCESS: Only you can judge it, father.

SCHWEINSHREKKER: Hopeless!

BELICANTA: Next.

KING: Someone else has come to torment me?

BELICANTA: God has spoken. God has revealed
The music with which the King can be healed.
God will do all that God can
Through the gifts of a holy man.
Enter FRIAR with Sausage Drum.

SCHWEINSHREKKER: That Friar! That lunatic!
That bellyful of moonlight.
Keep that keg away from the King!

BELICANTA: The Musical Contest . . .

[129]

SCHWEINSHREKKER: Is over! It's closed.
And if that Friar . . .
FRIAR *hits* SCHWEINSHREKKER *with sausage.*
BELICANTA: Begin, dear.
FRIAR: Downcast is the King of Illness.
That is Hell on Earth.
But the Belly conquers him
With puddings and with mirth.

With sausages and merriment
We'll conquer him or die.
So drink and feast and drink again
Unto our Lord on high.
KING: Enough! Enough!
Stop him.
When will you stop?
FRIAR: Downcast is the King . . .
That is Hell on Earth . . .
But the Belly conquers . . . conquers . . . conquers . . .
SCHWEINSHREKKER *hits the* FRIAR.
SCHWEINSHREKKER: Stop, you lunatic!
BELICANTA: Stop. Stop now, you fool,
Stop I say.
PRINCESS: Stop him.
Won't somebody stop him?
With his last blow SCHWEINSHREKKER *jumps on the*
singing FRIAR. *The* KING *pulls off his turban. He lurches*
from his throne and staggers. His feet are tiptoe hooves,
both his ears are great pig's ears.
KING: Find that pig! Search night and day.
Arrest every swineherd. Kill every curly-tailed grunting
creature in my kingdom.
Slaughter them all, large and small.

Slaughter them!
Slaughter them!
(*to* FRIAR) Find that pig or be executed.
Exit.

SCHWEINSHREKKER: The contest was a failure.
Exit.

PRINCESS: If that Schweinshrekker catches Otto and little
Marigold,
He will torture them to death.
Exit.

FRIAR: Somewhere in this world
Smiling sits the cure
For every ailment . . .
BELICANTA *hits* FRIAR *with sausage.*

BELICANTA: Fool!
Exit.

FRIAR: . . . Man can endure.
Exit.

[*Musical Transition.*]

SCENE 8

Enter OTTO, *ripping off his disguise.* PIGLETS *follow
excitedly.*

OTTO: Like the tree in its leaf
Like the sun in its skies
I'm sick of disguise.
I don't care what happens,
She said she loved me.
She said it. And I heard it.
I have come to the Palace
To stand at the walls

To shout at the windows
Princess, Princess, I love you!
So let your father chop off my head,
I shall love you for ever.

Marigold, Orange-blossom,
Come along, my beauty, and bring your curly tail,
The Sun is on a journey and the Moon is in full sail.
Honeysuckle, Snowdrop,
Where are you?
Best behaviour in the King's Palace.
Rose-petal, Meadowsweet,
  . . . Of all God's flowers the little pig
Is prettiest of all.
OTTO *comforts his piglets.* FRIAR *emerges.*
FRIAR: Caught bare-faced! Kissing a pig!
    The King has put a reward on your head
    And on the heads of all your pigs.
OTTO: O man of God, look the other way
    I'll be my own true self some other day.
FRIAR: No, no. Now I know who you are
    How could I hide the Truth?
    Your pigs or your life, your pigs or your life.
    Ha, now I have you and I have your pigs.
    Your pigs or your life.
OTTO: You are God's servant.
    What will He think?
FRIAR: God must eat and so must his servants.
    A dead man cannot pray.
    And a hungry man is a kitchen of devils.
    Your pigs or your life. And I want them all.
    Ah what beauties! What luscious plumplings!
    (PIGLETS *squeal.*)

Look at that delicious little darling!

OTTO: My pigs are my children.

FRIAR: Ah what succulents!

What a heavenly rascal, that one!

(FRIAR *prods a* PIGLET *with his staff,* PIGLET *utters a*
perfect note.)

What did I hear?

(FRIAR *prods another, and gets another perfect note.*)

Pork with perfect pitch?

(FRIAR *goes on prodding, to perfect notes.*)

Are they all bewitched?

Or is this a musical breed?

Have you interbred them

With nightingales or thrushes?

(FRIAR *prods out a melody.*)

I see the King is right.

And you have bewitched him

With a spellbinding pig.

(FRIAR *plays the* PIGLETS, '*The Pig Organ*'.)

A revelation!

God has spoken to me

Out of the mouths of piglets and sucklings.

These pigs shall be my instrument to cure the King.

I shall be Court Musician.

These piglets are a natural organ.

OTTO: These piglets are nobody's organ.

FRIAR: Yes, you heard. An organ-heard.

OTTO: An organ-herd?

FRIAR: Yes, an organ herd.

OTTO: You cannot take my pigs.

Enter SCHWEINSHREKKER.

SCHWEINSHREKKER: You are under arrest. Fraternizing
with pigs!

[133]

And all your pigs are under arrest.
Every pig in the kingdom is under arrest.
To be a pig is a major treason
Punishable by death.
Hands on your heads and your mouths shut.

FRIAR: You shall be punished.

SCHWEINSHREKKER: I shall be promoted.

OTTO: Dead or alive, I shall be near the Princess.

SCENE 9

Enter BELICANTA.

BELICANTA: Murderer! I see you! Devil! Sorcerer!
That pig killed my husband!
You are a witch! That's your pig!
And you have bewitched it!
Scream offstage. Enter KING *followed by the* PRINCESS.
[*Finale – Sextetto:*]

KING: What do I smell?
What do I see?
Do I see what I see?
I see the sun
Asleep on a cloud –
And it is a PIG!
I see the Moon
Rooting up the stars –
And it is a PIG!
I see Heaven
Open wide –
I see – a PIG!

OTTO: Princess, Princess!

PRINCESS: Otto, Otto!
Please, a miracle for Otto.

Something miraculous!
Something impossible!
A miracle for father!
A miracle for Otto!

SCHWEINSHREKKER: The King's brain is cracking.
Pig is forbidden, pig is forbidden.
He'll be the death of the King.

KING: I see hosts of pigs.

FRIAR: He that hath ears let him hear.
Angels sing in the pigsty and no man may hear them sing.
I bring the Music to cure the King.
These pigs are not what they seem.
They are musical instruments
Of the most heavenly make.
Order, you beasts! Sing, you brutes!
What's got into your pigs?

OTTO *and* PRINCESS: Don't frighten them. Don't frighten them.

FRIAR: Sing, you brats! Sing, sing, sing!

BELICANTA: What can you expect from pigs?
O I could wring their necks
If they had necks.

SCWEINSHREKKER: They'll be the death of the King.
Look – he's cracking up!
Get that religious haggis out of here!

FRIAR: Sing, or I'll roast you till you sing with sizzle!
Sing, sing, sing.
Listen to this, Your Majesty!
(*The more the* FRIAR *prods and belabours the* PIGLETS,
the more they squeal and mill around in panic.)
Why won't they sing?
Pig panic reaches a crescendo.

SCHWEINSHREKKER: Look at the King!

[135]

PRINCESS: Father!

Great silence. The KING *reveals himself totally as a pig.*

KING: I am a pig! I am a PIG!

ALL: The King is a pig! The King is a pig!

PRINCESS: Please God let it all be a dream.

I am asleep and this is a dream.

BELICANTA: My husband is dead and the King is a pig!

Pigs are people and people are pigs!

Pigs! People! People! Pigs!

My head will burst!

FRIAR: Happy is the man whom God correcteth

He shall be plunged into the ditch

His dwelling shall be with the beasts of the field.

SCHWEINSHREKKER (*to* FRIAR): Hang him! Hang him! He can't heal souls!

He calls God and gets the Devil!

His God is the gut! His God is the gut!

Witchdoctor!

During OTTO's *song the* PIGLETS *become calm and the general chaos dies away.*

OTTO: O pretty is the little pig

As pretty as a flower

As pink as the pink rose

In the rose-bower

Is this Princess Isca or

A girl who tends the swine?

Blessed Queen of Beauty

You shall be mine.

BELICANTA: Like a flute on a mountain

Or a comb through my hair

This song touches my soul

And sets peace there.

FRIAR: Eating drinking I have known
    Miracles of the tongue!
    But never before mad pigs
    Becalmed with such a song!
SCHWEINSHREKKER: I've sleepwalked my life away –
    Snoring medicine!
    At last a song opens my eyes
    And the light comes in.
PRINCESS: No magic on earth, no magic below
    Or in the heavens above
    But a mighty Demon
    And his name is Love.

    And his speech is music
    And his work is the birth
    Of all living lovely things
    Here on this earth.
OTTO: And her speech is music
    And her work is the birth
    Of all living lovely things
    Here on this earth.
    The KING *reveals himself, transformed to his original*
    appearance.
KING: What happened to me?
    I have been in Hell.
    I have had a nightmare
    Too hideous to tell.

    A giant boar drank from my skull
    My soul was his wine.
    All around me hell was roasting
    Howling swine.

    Then the heavens began to sing

And through the infernal fire
This young man came for me
With his heavenly choir!

OTTO: My song was only earthly till
A dove from heaven brought it Love and Light.

KING: Your song has transformed us.
This is my Court Musician!

OTTO: Here is my music. Here is my magic.
Here is all the love I sing with.

KING (*to* PRINCESS): Take his hand!

OTTO: And this is my orchestra.

KING: A miracle of piglets!
My reign has been blessed
With a miracle. Rejoice!

ALL: A miracle! A miracle!
A miracle of piglets!
Rejoice! Rejoice!
During the FRIAR's *song* BELICANTA *and*
SCHWEINSHREKKER *adorn the heads of the* PIGLETS
with laurel crowns.

FRIAR: Downcast is the King of Illness
That is Hell on Earth
But the Belly conquers him
With puddings and with mirth.

With sausages and merriment
We'll conquer him or die
So drink and feast and drink again
Unto our Lord on high.